EMBRACING JESUS' LOVE

Jesus Calling Bible Study Series

Jesus Always Bible Study Series

JESUS ALWAYS BIBLE STUDY SERIES

EMBRACING
JESUS' LOVE

EIGHT SESSIONS

with Karen Lee-Thorp

THOMAS NELSON
Since 1798

Published in Nashville, Tennessee, by Thomas Nelson. Thomas Nelson is a registered trademark of HarperCollins Christian Publishing, Inc.

ISBN 978-0-310-09134-9

First Printing January 2018 / Printed in the United States of America

CONTENTS

INTRODUCTION

Sometimes our busy and difficult lives give us the impression that God is silent. We cry out to Him, but our feelings tell us He isn't answering our prayers. In this, our feelings are incorrect. God hears the prayers of His children and speaks directly into the situations in which we find ourselves. The trouble is that our lives are often too hectic, our minds too distracted, for us to take in what He offers.

This *Jesus Always* Bible study is designed to help individuals and groups meditate on the words of Scripture and hear them not just as words said to people long ago but as words said to us today in the here and now. The goal is to help the heart open up and respond to what the mind reads—to encounter the living God as He speaks through the Scriptures. The writer to the Hebrews tells us:

> In the past God spoke to our ancestors through the prophets at many times and in various ways, but in these last days he has spoken to us by his Son, whom he appointed heir of all things, and through whom also he made the universe. The Son is the radiance of God's glory and the exact representation of his being, sustaining all things by his powerful word.
>
> —HEBREWS 1:1–3

God has spoken to us through His Son, Jesus Christ. The New Testament gives us the chance to walk with Jesus, see what He does, and hear Him speak into the sometimes-confusing situations in which we find ourselves. The Old Testament tells the story of how God prepared a people to be the family of Jesus, and in the experiences of those men and women, we find our own lives mirrored.

THE GOAL OF THIS SERIES

The *Jesus Always Bible Study Series* offers you a chance to lay down your cares, enter God's Presence, and hear Him speak through His Word. You will get to spend some time silently studying a passage of Scripture, and then, if you're meeting with a group, openly sharing your insights and hearing what others discovered. You'll also get to discuss excerpts from the *Jesus Always* devotional that relate to the themes of the Bible passages. In this way, you will learn how to better make space in your life for the Spirit of God to speak to you through the Word of God and the people of God.

THE FLOW OF EACH SESSION

Each session of this study guide contains the following elements:

- CONSIDER IT. The two questions in this opening section serve as an icebreaker to help you start thinking about the theme of the session, connecting it to your own past or present experience, and allowing you to get to know the others in your group more deeply. If you've had a busy day and your mind is full of distractions, these questions can help you better focus.

- EXPERIENCE IT. Here you will find two readings from *Jesus Always* along with some questions for reflection. This is your chance to talk with others about the biblical principles found within the *Jesus Always* devotions. Can you relate to what each reading describes? What insights from God's Word does it illuminate? What does it motivate you to do? This section will assist you in applying these biblical principles to your everyday habits.

- STUDY IT. Next you'll explore a Scripture passage connected to the session topic and the readings from *Jesus Always.* You will not only analyze these Bible passages but also pray through them in ways designed to engage your heart and your head. You'll first talk with your group about what the verse or verses mean and then spend several minutes in silence, letting God speak into your life through His Word.

- LIVE IT. Finally, you will find five days' worth of suggested Scripture passages that you can pray through on your own during the week. Suggested questions for additional study and reflection are provided.

FOR LEADERS

If you are leading a group through this study guide, please see the Leader's Notes at the end of the guide. You'll find background on the design of the study as well as suggested answers for some of the study questions.

SESSION 1

INSEPARABLE LOVE

CONSIDER IT

In a fallen world, separation is a part of life. We can lose a parent to death or divorce. We can lose a best friend or a beloved pet. We can lose a job, a spouse, even a child. Everything was good a year ago, and now it seems like a tank has rolled through our yard and into our house.

Jesus understands how these losses affect us. He doesn't minimize them. Yet instead of shielding His followers from the losses, He promises that we will have His love to hold onto in the midst of them and that nothing can ever separate us from His love. Friends and even family may turn away from us, but Jesus never will. That's the first thing we need to know about His love: it's *inseparable* from us. It will never go away. Nothing can drive a wedge between His love and His people. Not even the pain we feel when we lose something precious.

In this session, we'll explore this truth to see if we can let it sink into the depths of our souls. We need to have this assurance as bedrock certainty, so that when trouble comes we won't be devastated by it.

1. *When you were a child, what was something you lost that you loved?*

2. *How has that loss affected you as an adult?*

EXPERIENCE IT

Nothing in all creation can separate you from My Love. Pause and ponder what an astonishing promise this is! You live in a world where separations abound: wives from husbands, children from parents, friends from friends, childhood dreams from adult realities. But there is one terrible separation you will never have to face: isolation from My loving Presence.

I want you to cling to Me with tenacious confidence. This gives you strength to cope with the uncertainties of living in such a broken, unstable world. Anxious thoughts can assault your mind and fill you with fear if you forget that My Love will never fail you. When you find yourself feeling afraid, grasp My hand in childlike trust. Rest in the protection of My Presence, and remember that *perfect Love drives out fear.*

The greatest wealth on earth is minuscule compared with the riches of My boundless Love. Yet this is My free gift to all who follow Me. *How priceless is My unfailing Love!*

—FROM *JESUS ALWAYS*, MARCH 17

3. *If you are a child of God, what helps you believe that nothing can separate you from His love?*

_____

_____

_____

4. *How easy is it for you to cling to Jesus with confidence? Why do you think that's the case?*

_____

_____

_____

Let My unfailing Love be your comfort. One definition of "comfort" is a person or thing that makes you feel less upset or frightened during a time of trouble. Because you live in such a broken world, trouble is never far away. There are many sources of comfort in the world, yet only one of them is unfailing: My Love! Other sources will help you *some* of the time, but My tender Presence is with you *all* of the time.

My perfect, inexhaustible Love is not just a *thing* that makes you feel less upset; it's also a *Person. Nothing in all creation can separate you from Me.* And *I* am inseparable from My Love.

As My cherished follower, you can turn to Me for comfort at all times. Since you have this boundless Source of blessing—*Me*—I want you to be a blessing in the lives of other people. You *can comfort those in any trouble with the comfort you have received from Me.*

—FROM *JESUS ALWAYS*, FEBRUARY 14

5. *When is a time in your life that you received comfort from God?*

_____

_____

_____

_____

6. *When is a time in your life when you had the chance to comfort someone else? (Share your experience without revealing any identifying information about the person.) How did the opportunity affect you?*

_____

_____

_____

_____

STUDY IT

Read aloud the following passage from Romans 8:31–39. As you do, note that the apostle Paul has been describing for his readers the many wondrous things that are true of those who are united with Christ: God's Spirit prays for them in their weakness. God works all things together for their highest good. Even their sufferings aren't worth comparing to the glory that is their destiny (see verses 26–30). Paul now wraps up this section of his letter with a crescendo of good news. "Justifies" in verse 33 means to be declared not guilty. Also, Paul isn't speaking glibly about suffering in verses 35–36; he has experienced plenty of trouble, hardships, and persecution in his efforts to spread the news of Christ across a hostile and dangerous empire.

[31] What, then, shall we say in response to these things? If God is for us, who can be against us? [32] He who did not spare his own Son, but gave him up for us all—how will he not also, along with him, graciously give us all things? [33] Who will bring any charge against those whom God has chosen? It is God who justifies. [34] Who then is the one who condemns? No one. Christ Jesus who died—more than that, who was raised to life—is at the right hand of God and is also interceding for us. [35] Who shall separate us from the love of Christ? Shall trouble or hardship or persecution or famine or nakedness or danger or sword? [36] As it is written:

> "For your sake we face death all day long;
> we are considered as sheep to be slaughtered."

[37] No, in all these things we are more than conquerors through him who loved us. [38] For I am convinced that neither death nor life, neither angels nor demons, neither the present nor the future, nor any powers, [39] neither height nor depth, nor anything else in all creation, will be able to separate us from the love of God that is in Christ Jesus our Lord.

7. *What does it mean that God is "for" those who follow Him (see verse 31)?*

8. *Paul writes, "It is God who justifies. Who then is the one who condemns?" (verses 33–34). As a believer, does being declared "not guilty" for your faults make you feel loved? Or do you have a strong inner accusing voice that feeds a sense of guilt? Explain.*

9. *Paul doesn't say God will take away His children's sufferings in this life. He says their sufferings can't separate them from His love. Is that good news for you? Or do you tend to feel separated from God's love when you suffer?*

10. *How does it affect you to know that Jesus is at the right hand of the Father, interceding for those who follow Him (see verse 34)?*

11. What are the things that threaten to separate you from God's love, or that feel like they are already separating you?

_____

_____

_____

_____

12. Take two minutes of silence to reread the passage, looking for a sentence, phrase, or even one word that stands out as something Jesus may want you to focus on in your life. If you're meeting with a group, the leader will keep track of time. At the end of two minutes, you may share with the group the word or phrase that came to you in the silence.

_____

_____

_____

_____

13. Read the passage aloud again. Take another two minutes of silence, prayerfully considering what response God might want you to make to what you have read in His Word. If you're meeting with a group, the leader will again keep track of time. At the end of two minutes, you may share with the group what came to you in the silence if you wish.

_____

_____

_____

_____

14. *If you're meeting with a group, how can the members pray for you? If you're using this study on your own, what would you like to say to God right now?*

Live It

At the end of each session you'll find suggested Scripture readings for spending time alone with God during five days of the coming week. This week, the theme of each reading focuses on God's love in Paul's letters. Read each passage slowly, pausing to think about what is being said. Rather than approaching this as an assignment to complete, think of it as an opportunity to meet with the One who loves you most. Use any of the questions that are helpful.

Day 1

Read Romans 5:5. Why can believers in Christ have confidence about their future?

If you are a follower of Christ, how have you experienced God pouring His love into your heart? How does this affect what you think and do?

Sometimes we expect God's love to feel grand or extravagant. How do you think different people experience God's love in different ways?

Thank God today for pouring out His love into your heart. If you don't feel God's love, ask Him to make its presence real to you.

Day 2

Read Romans 5:6–8. How has God demonstrated His extravagant love for us?

How much of an impact does that have on you? Are you gripped by what God has done, or does it seem more of an abstract idea? Why do you suppose that's the case?

Sometimes you may not feel gripped by God's generosity because you don't feel like you were such a "bad" sinner in the first place. How aware of your sin are you—your sin in the past and in the present? Explain.

Take some time today to gratefully reflect on some of your sins for which Christ died. Think about where you would be now without Him.

Day 3

Read Ephesians 2:1–7. In verses 1–3, how does Paul describe the state of sin?

If you're a believer, how does that help you picture what you would be like if Christ hadn't involved Himself in your life?

In your own words, how does Paul describe the way God has loved those who believe in Him in verses 4–7?

Do something today to express your gratitude for God's love in sending Christ for you.

Day 4

Read Galatians 2:20. How does Paul describe what has happened to those who follow Christ because of His love?

Can you honestly say, "I no longer live, but Christ lives in me"? What does that mean to you?

If you're a Christian, what is something you have done because you live by faith in Jesus?

Today, ponder what has happened to you because Christ gave Himself for you—or what could be different in your life if you chose to follow Him.

Day 5

Read Ephesians 5:1–2. How does Paul want you to follow God's example?

_____

_____

_____

Why does this matter? Why isn't it enough to just be grateful for what Jesus has done?

_____

_____

_____

How could you have followed God's example yesterday? Did you do it?

_____

_____

_____

When you see a chance to "walk in the way of love" today, seize it.

EVERLASTING LOVE

CONSIDER IT

Depending on how far along you are in your walk with God, your love for the people around you will be like a puddle, or a swimming pool, or a pond, or maybe—if you're one of the great saints—like a lake. In any case, that "water" has boundaries. It is contained; it only takes up so much space; it hasn't always been there; and the water levels are likely to rise and fall depending on your mood and whether the people around you displease you in some way.

God's love is different. When He says it is "an everlasting love" (Jeremiah 31:3), He means it is like an ocean without a shore. It began in eternity and will go on for eternity. If we have pledged ourselves to Him, there's no risk that His love for us will end if we displease Him. After all, He loved us before we were born, He has loved us through all the years of our lukewarmness and self-absorption, and Jesus died for us at our worst.

In this session, we will stick a toe into that ocean and attempt to wrap our minds around this promise of everlasting love.

1. *When you were growing up, did you have unconditional, boundless love from your parents? Or was their love for you limited in some way? Briefly describe your experience.*

2. *How do you think your experience of your parents' love affects your ability to connect with God's everlasting love for you?*

EXPERIENCE IT

I call you by name and lead you. I know you—I know every detail about you. You are never a number or statistic to Me; My involvement in your life is far more personal and intimate than you can comprehend. So *follow Me* with a glad heart.

After My resurrection, when Mary Magdalene mistook Me for the gardener, I spoke one word: *"Mary."*

Hearing Me say her name, she recognized Me and *cried out in Aramaic, "Rabboni!" (which means Teacher).*

Beloved, I also speak *your* name in the depths of your spirit. When you read your Bible, try inserting your name into appropriate passages. Remember: *I called you out of darkness into My marvelous Light.* I chose to set My *everlasting Love* upon you. Take time to "hear" Me speaking to you personally in Scripture, reassuring you of My Love. The unshakable knowledge that I love you forever provides a firm foundation for your life. It strengthens you so that you can follow Me faithfully and joyfully—*proclaiming My praises* as you journey through your life.

—FROM *JESUS ALWAYS,* JANUARY 19

3. *In John 10:3, Jesus says that "he calls his own sheep by name and leads them out." What does this mean for the members of His family?*

_____

_____

_____

4. *What are some ways you can interact more personally with God through Scripture?*

_____

_____

_____

The Light of My Presence shines on every situation in your life—past, present, and future. I knew you *before the creation of the world*, and *I have loved you with an everlasting Love*. You are never alone, so look for Me in your moments. Search for Me as for hidden treasure.

Seek to "see" Me in the midst of all your circumstances; don't let them obscure your view of Me. Sometimes I display My Presence in grand, glorious ways. At other times I show Myself in simple, humble ways that make sense only to you. Ask Me to open your eyes and your heart to discern *all* My communications to you, beloved.

As you go through this day, remind yourself to look for the Light of My Presence shining on your life. Don't have such a narrow focus that you see only responsibilities and worldly concerns. Instead, expand your focus to include *Me* in your perspective. *You will seek Me and find Me when you search for Me with all your heart.*

—FROM *JESUS ALWAYS*, AUGUST 29

5. *When have you "seen" God's presence in the midst of your circumstances?*

_____

_____

_____

_____

6. *Are there any circumstances in your life that have caused you to doubt that God loves you with an everlasting love?*

_____

_____

_____

_____

STUDY IT

Read aloud the following passage from Jeremiah 31:3–6. In the chapters preceding these verses, the prophet Jeremiah has predicted the Babylonians will destroy the nation of Judah just as the Assyrians destroyed her northern sister, Israel, and take the people of Judah (the Jews) into exile. The Lord sent this destruction as punishment for His people's rebellion against Him. But now, He gives Jeremiah a series of prophecies that look to a time beyond the exile, when He will restore His people to their land. As you read these verses, note that a *timbrel* is like a tambourine. Samaria and Ephraim are regions in what used to be Israel. Zion is Jerusalem, where the Lord's temple stood until the Babylonians reduced it to rubble.

³ The LORD appeared to us in the past, saying:

"I have loved you with an everlasting love;
    I have drawn you with unfailing kindness.
⁴ I will build you up again,
    and you, Virgin Israel, will be rebuilt.
Again you will take up your timbrels
    and go out to dance with the joyful.
⁵ Again you will plant vineyards
    on the hills of Samaria;
the farmers will plant them
    and enjoy their fruit.
⁶ There will be a day when watchmen cry out
    on the hills of Ephraim,
'Come, let us go up to Zion,
    to the LORD our God.'"

7. *Why is it important to know that the Lord's love is everlasting (see verse 3), especially when we are guilty of sin?*

_____

_____

_____

8. *The phrase "unfailing kindness" (verse 3) is from a Hebrew word that means "loyal love." This is a love that does whatever it should for the other person's good without first calculating, "What's in it for me?" How have you received that kind of love from God?*

_____

_____

_____

9. *Imagine yourself taking up a tambourine and going out to dance with the joyful. Would that be in character for you? Or would people be surprised to see you like that? Why did you answer the way you did?*

_____

_____

_____

10. *What would be the equivalent for you of planting vineyards and enjoying their fruit (see verse 5)?*

_____

_____

_____

11. *Jeremiah foresees a time when God's people will again live in Ephraim (part of the Promised Land) and be both able and eager to worship in Jerusalem the way they were meant to do (see verse 6). How is the opportunity to gather with others to worship God a profound blessing that shouldn't be taken for granted?*

_____

_____

_____

12. *Take two minutes of silence to reread the passage, looking for a sentence, phrase, or even one word that stands out as something Jesus may want you to focus on in your life. If you're meeting with a group, the leader will keep track of time. At the end of two minutes, you may share with the group the word or phrase that came to you in the silence.*

_____

_____

_____

13. *Read the passage aloud again. Take another two minutes of silence, prayerfully considering what response God might want you to make to what you have read in His Word. If you're meeting with a group, the leader will again keep track of time. At the end of two minutes, you may share with the group what came to you in the silence if you wish.*

_____

_____

_____

14. *If you're meeting with a group, how can the members pray for you? If you're using this study on your own, what would you like to say to God right now?*

_____

_____

_____

LIVE IT

This week's readings are focused on the theme of God's unfailing love. Read each passage slowly, pausing to think about what is being said. Rather than approaching this as an assignment to complete, think of it as an opportunity to meet with the One who loves you most. Use any of the questions that are helpful.

Day 1

Read Psalm 6:4. This verse uses a Hebrew word that is frequent in the Old Testament and is translated as unfailing or steadfast love, loving-kindness, mercy, kindness, or loyalty. Why is the psalmist in need of God's unfailing love?

_____

_____

_____

_____

Why are you in need of God's unfailing love today?

_____

_____

_____

How have you experienced God's unfailing love in the past?

_____

_____

_____

Today, ask God to save you—from whatever threatens you—because of His unfailing love.

Day 2

Read Psalm 13:3–5. What does the psalmist request of God in this passage?

_____

_____

_____

How does the psalmist express his faith in God's deliverance (see verse 5)?

_____

_____

_____

What threatening situations are you facing today? How can you choose to trust in God's unfailing love in spite of what you are confronting?

_____

_____

_____

Today, look for opportunities to trust in God's unfailing love.

Day 3

Read Psalm 26:2–4. What difference does God's unfailing love make in your life?

_____

_____

_____

Why would being mindful of God's unfailing love keep you from associating with liars and hypocrites (verse 4)?

_____

_____

_____

How can you keep God's unfailing love at the front of your mind today?

_____

_____

_____

Set up a reminder of some kind, such as on your phone, to reflect on God's unfailing love in your life.

Day 4

Read Psalm 33:5. Give a few examples of how the earth is full of the Lord's unfailing love.

_____

_____

_____

What are some of the things in the world that tempt you to doubt that His unfailing love is everywhere?

_____

_____

_____

How would your life be better if you truly believed the earth is full of the Lord's unfailing love?

_____

_____

_____

Today, watch for signs of God's unfailing love taking place all around you.

Day 5

Read Psalm 33:18. What does it mean to place your hope in God's unfailing love?

_____

_____

_____

Biblical hope is a confident expectation. Do you have a confident expectation? If so, for what? If not, why not?

_____

_____

_____

Why is it important to ground your hope in God's unfailing love?

_____

_____

_____

_____

Let the small evidences of God's unfailing love that you notice around you remind you to place your hope in Him.

ABOUNDING LOVE

CONSIDER IT

When we speak of God's love as *everlasting*, we are talking about the fact that it is infinite in time—He has always loved us and will always love us. When we speak of it as *abounding* love, we are reflecting on its infinite measure. He doesn't just love us moderately. His love for us is extreme. It wells up, overflows, and fills the universe. No matter how much we mess up, when we confess and seek His forgiveness, His love is more than enough to restore us.

Compared to God, the love we have for others is mediocre. We may be enthralled with another person—counting the time until we can be together again, thinking constantly of him or her, wishing we could be nearer—but God's love is so much greater. His love for His children is more than mere emotion; it is a conscious choice that He promises to honor forever.

In this session, we will revel in that abounding love. We will consider what it takes to trust in such love—to lean all our weight on this pure love that will never collapse or weaken. We are made of mere dust, and yet God treasures us as if we were made of diamonds. Let's see if we can let that sink in today.

1. *How have you experienced God's love during the past week?*

2. *Did you recognize it as God's love at the time? Or are you only identifying it as that in hindsight? Why do you suppose that's the case?*

EXPERIENCE IT

Great is My Love, reaching to the heavens; My faithfulness reaches to the skies. You can feel wonderfully secure in Love that has no boundaries or limits. My faithfulness also has no bounds. Respond to these wondrous gifts with worship. The more you praise Me, the more you can *reflect My Glory* to other people. This is the work of the Holy Spirit, who is *transforming you into My likeness with ever-increasing Glory.* As you draw near Me through worship, I change you profoundly, equipping you to make Me known to others.

My Love not only reaches to the heavens but descends upon you from heavenly realms. Keep looking up to Me, beloved. See Me smiling on you in radiant approval. My limitless Love falls continually upon you, like heavenly snowflakes that melt into your upturned face. No matter how distressing your circumstances, this Love is sufficient to sustain you. Someday you will even ascend to heaven on it. I eagerly anticipate the time when *I will take you into Glory*—to be with Me forever!

—FROM *JESUS ALWAYS,* APRIL 10

3. *Worship is a matter of choosing to praise God more than it is a matter of your emotions. How readily do you choose to worship the God of boundless love, whether in community or one-on-one with Jesus? What helps you? What hinders you?*

_____

_____

_____

4. *What is the connection between our feelings and our worship? How can worship increase our security in God's abounding love?*

_____

_____

_____

I meet you in the place of your deepest need. So come to Me just as you are, leaving pretense and performance behind. You are totally transparent to Me: I know everything about you. Yet because you are My own—redeemed by My blood—I have unlimited, unfailing Love for you.

Ask My Spirit to help you be honest and open with Me. Don't be ashamed of your neediness; instead, use it to connect with Me in humble dependence. Invite Me to have My way in your life. Remember that *I am the Potter, and you are the clay.* The weakness you bring Me is malleable in My hands, and I use it to mold you according to My will.

Your deepest need is to *lean on, trust in, and be confident in Me.* Accepting your lack of strength helps you lean on Me in unashamed dependence. I am training you to trust Me *with all your heart and mind*—a lifelong endeavor. And the best way to *not be afraid* is to have confidence in Me, *your Strength.*

—FROM *JESUS ALWAYS*, MAY 9

5. *Why do you think it's hard for some people to leave all pretense and performance behind and go to God with their needs?*

_____

_____

_____

_____

6. *Why do you think some people feel so negative about their neediness?*

_____

_____

_____

_____

STUDY IT

Read aloud the following passage Psalm 103:1–18. As you do, note that the word "praise" in verses 1 and 2 literally means "bless." God has showered us with blessings, and we respond by giving blessing back to Him. The word "pit" in verse 4 can mean the grave or death, or it can mean the depths of despair. When the psalmist says God "heals all your diseases" (verse 3), he doesn't mean that God promises to heal every believer of every physical ailment. Rather, he means that every healing comes ultimately from God, who will heal us permanently after death. The word "covenant" in verse 18 refers to a relational bond cemented by promises.

[1] Praise the LORD, my soul;
   all my inmost being, praise his holy name.
[2] Praise the LORD, my soul,
   and forget not all his benefits—
[3] who forgives all your sins
   and heals all your diseases,
[4] who redeems your life from the pit
   and crowns you with love and compassion,
[5] who satisfies your desires with good things
   so that your youth is renewed like the eagle's.
[6] The LORD works righteousness
   and justice for all the oppressed.
[7] He made known his ways to Moses,
   his deeds to the people of Israel:
[8] The LORD is compassionate and gracious,
   slow to anger, abounding in love.
[9] He will not always accuse,
   nor will he harbor his anger forever;
[10] he does not treat us as our sins deserve
   or repay us according to our iniquities.
[11] For as high as the heavens are above the earth,
   so great is his love for those who fear him;

¹² as far as the east is from the west,
    so far has he removed our transgressions from us.
¹³ As a father has compassion on his children,
    so the Lord has compassion on those who fear him;
¹⁴ for he knows how we are formed,
    he remembers that we are dust.
¹⁵ The life of mortals is like grass,
    they flourish like a flower of the field;
¹⁶ the wind blows over it and it is gone,
    and its place remembers it no more.
¹⁷ But from everlasting to everlasting
    the Lord's love is with those who fear him,
    and his righteousness with their children's children—
¹⁸ with those who keep his covenant
    and remember to obey his precepts.

7. *What are some indications of God's abounding love that are listed in this psalm?*

_____

_____

_____

_____

8. *Which of these indications is most significant to you today? Why did you answer as you did?*

_____

_____

_____

_____

9. *When have you experienced some indication of God's abounding love? How have you responded?*

10. *God has compassion for us because He knows we are "dust" (see verse 14). What does this mean to you? Why is it important that He remembers this about us?*

11. *If we are only dust, how can the Lord's love for His followers be with them "from everlasting to everlasting" (verse 17)?*

12. *Take two minutes of silence to reread the passage, looking for a sentence, phrase, or even one word that stands out as something Jesus may want you to focus on in your life. If you're meeting with a group, the leader will keep track of time. At the end of two minutes, you may share with the group the word or phrase that came to you in the silence.*

13. *Read the passage aloud again. Take another two minutes of silence, prayerfully considering what response God might want you to make to what you have read in His Word. If you're meeting with a group, the leader will again keep track of time. At the end of two minutes, you may share with the group what came to you in the silence if you wish.*

14. *If you're meeting with a group, how can the members pray for you? If you're using this study on your own, what would you like to say to God right now?*

LIVE IT

This week's readings will focus on the theme of God's abounding love. Read each passage slowly, pausing to think about what is being said. Rather than approaching this as an assignment to complete, think of it as an opportunity to meet with the One who loves you most. Use any of the questions that are helpful.

Day 1

Read Exodus 34:5–7. These verses relate what happened when Moses asked to see God's glory. What strikes you most about what the Lord says about His essential nature?

_____

_____

_____

How do you think the Lord can be both "abounding in love" and yet punish sin over generations?

_____

_____

_____

Where do you think the sacrifice of Jesus on the cross fits in with God's essential nature expressed here?

_____

_____

_____

Today, take a few moments to reflect on God's nature and what that means to you.

Day 2

Read Nehemiah 9:16–21. In this passage, Nehemiah is praying and recalling what God did for his ancestors. According to Nehemiah, how did God demonstrate His abounding love?

Can you identify with any of these ways of experiencing God's abounding love? If so, how have you experienced something similar?

Why is it helpful to remember the ways God showed His abounding love to people in past generations? How does it benefit us to reflect on things that may have happened long ago?

Thank God today for allowing His children to be included in the lineage of those who have benefited from His abounding love.

Day 3

Read Psalm 86:4–5. The psalmist says the Lord is abounding in love to all who call on Him. Do you think you lose that benefit if you are too busy to call on Him? Why did you answer the way you did?

How is trust relevant to benefiting from God's abounding love?

How do you need God's abounding love today?

Tell God something for which you need His forgiveness today, and then relax in confidence in His abounding love for you.

Day 4

Read Joel 2:13. It was customary in Joel's day for people to rip their clothes as a sign of grief. What would it mean to "rend your heart"?

Why would rending your heart be more important to God than rending your clothes?

How is God's abounding love a motivation to rend your heart?

Do something today that shows your gratitude for God's gift of forgiveness.

Day 5

Read Philippians 1:8–10. How does this passage about abounding love differ from the ones you have been reading on previous days?

How is our abounding love connected to God's abounding love?

Why are knowledge and depth of insight (or understanding) important features of real love?

Ask God today to give you love that abounds in knowledge and depth of insight.

COMPASSIONATE LOVE

CONSIDER IT

Leprosy is a contagious disease that used to be incurable and fatal, so it was common to exile sufferers to leper colonies. One such colony was located on the island of Molokai in Hawaii. In 1873, a Belgian priest named Damien De Veuster went to the colony to minister to the physical and spiritual needs of the sufferers. Along with native volunteers, Damien built homes, roads, schools, churches, hospitals—even graves and coffins. He shared meals with the afflicted to show his care for them. Eventually, he contracted leprosy himself. He died of it in 1889.

Not everybody appreciated Damien. Some in the colony wanted a native priest, and in 1878, they requested that he be replaced. But he was the priest they got—a rough but caring man who was willing to go to the extreme to suffer with the people.

The word "compassion" literally means "to suffer with." Whenever God's children suffer, the Lord promises to be with them. He doesn't always make the suffering go away—and there may be times when we wish we had someone else to minister to us. But He is the God we have. He was willing to go to the extreme by becoming one of us and dying under the weight of our sin. In this session, we will reflect on God's compassionate love.

1. *When have you experienced compassion?*

2. *Why do we all need compassion?*

EXPERIENCE IT

Beloved, *My compassions never fail. They are new every morning.* So you can begin each day confidently, knowing that My vast reservoir of blessings is full to the brim. This knowledge helps you *wait for Me,* entrusting your long-unanswered prayers into My care and keeping. I assure you that not one of those petitions has slipped past Me unnoticed. I want you to drink deeply from My fountain of limitless Love and unfailing compassion. As you wait in My Presence, these divine nutrients are freely available to you.

Although many of your prayers are not yet answered, you can find hope in *My great faithfulness.* I keep all My promises in My perfect way and timing. I have promised to *give you Peace* that can displace the trouble and fear in your heart. If you become weary of waiting, remember that I also wait—*that I may be gracious to you and have mercy on you.* I hold back till you're ready to receive the things I have lovingly prepared for you. *Blessed are all those who wait for Me.*

—FROM *JESUS ALWAYS,* JULY 30

3. *In Lamentations 3:22, we read, "Because of the LORD's great love we are not consumed, for his compassions never fail." What does it mean to say that God's compassions never fail?*

_____

_____

_____

4. *How does knowing that God's love never fails for His children help you deal with unanswered prayer? How does it help you wait on Him for answers?*

_____

_____

_____

Though the mountains be shaken and the hills be removed, yet My unfail-ing Love for you will not be shaken nor My covenant of Peace be removed. Nothing on earth seems as enduring or immovable as soaring, majestic mountains. When you stand on their heights, breathing in that rarified air, you can almost smell eternity. Yet My Love and My Peace are even *more* enduring than the greatest mountain on earth!

Think deeply about *My unfailing Love.* One of the meanings of "unfailing" is *inexhaustible.* No matter how needy you are or how many times you fail Me, My supply of Love for you will never run low. Another meaning of "unfailing" is *constant.* I do not love you more on days when you perform well, nor do I love you less when you fail badly.

I Myself am your Peace. Live close to Me so you can enjoy this supernatural Peace. Come freely into My Presence, beloved, even when you're feeling bad about yourself. Remember who I am: *the Lord who has compassion on you.*

—FROM *JESUS ALWAYS,* JANUARY 25

5. *In Isaiah 54:10, God said to His people, "Though the mountains be shaken and the hills be removed, yet my unfailing love for you will not be shaken nor my covenant of peace be removed." What does this verse add to your thoughts about what it means to say that God's love is unfailing for those who have entrusted their lives to Him? How is this relevant to you?*

_____

_____

_____

6. *Are there times when it's hard for you to come freely into God's presence? If so, when are those times? What would help you?*

_____

_____

_____

Study It

Read aloud the following passage from Lamentations 3:19–33. In this biblical poem, the author (possibly the prophet Jeremiah) grieves over the destruction of Jerusalem by the Babylonians. It graphically depicts the suffering of the citizens of Jerusalem. The poet knows that God has allowed this suffering because His people have repeatedly and severely rebelled against Him and worshiped other gods. The climax of the poem—a glimpse of hope in the long lament—comes not at the end of the poem but in the very middle, in the second half of chapter 3, which we're going to study. When the poet speaks in verse 19 of his "wandering," he is referring to exile. After the Babylonians captured the city, they drove its surviving inhabitants out of their country and into other parts of the Babylonian Empire. Jeremiah went to Egypt.

19 I remember my affliction and my wandering,
   the bitterness and the gall.
20 I well remember them,
   and my soul is downcast within me.
21 Yet this I call to mind
   and therefore I have hope:
22 Because of the Lord's great love we are not consumed,
   for his compassions never fail.
23 They are new every morning;
   great is your faithfulness.
24 I say to myself, "The Lord is my portion;
   therefore I will wait for him."
25 The Lord is good to those whose hope is in him,
   to the one who seeks him;
26 it is good to wait quietly
   for the salvation of the Lord.
27 It is good for a man to bear the yoke
   while he is young.

²⁸ Let him sit alone in silence,
   for the LORD has laid it on him.
²⁹ Let him bury his face in the dust—
   there may yet be hope.
³⁰ Let him offer his cheek to one who would strike him,
   and let him be filled with disgrace.
³¹ For no one is cast off
   by the Lord forever.
³² Though he brings grief, he will show compassion,
   so great is his unfailing love.
³³ For he does not willingly bring affliction
   or grief to anyone.

7. *What reasons does this passage offer for hope in the midst of sorrow?*

_____

_____

_____

8. *How is it significant that these words of hope come in the middle of five chapters about loss and sorrow?*

_____

_____

_____

9. *This poet has lost his home, his property, and maybe all of his family and friends in the Babylonian invasion. But what does he realize he still has (see verse 22)?*

_____

_____

_____

10. *In verses 24–26, the poet describes how to go on with life after loss— in light of who God is. What do you think it means to say, "The Lord is my portion"? What does it mean to purposefully wait for God?*

11. *The poet's words in verse 33 could be translated, "It gives Him no pleasure to send affliction or grief." Even when God's people were rebellious and deserved to be punished, He didn't enjoy disciplining them. Neither does He enjoy allowing the afflictions or griefs of living in a fallen world. Why is this important for us to remember?*

12. *Take two minutes of silence to reread the passage, looking for a sentence, phrase, or even one word that stands out as something Jesus may want you to focus on in your life. If you're meeting with a group, the leader will keep track of time. At the end of two minutes, you may share with the group the word or phrase that came to you in the silence.*

13. *Read the passage aloud again. Take another two minutes of silence, prayerfully considering what response God might want you to make to what you have read in His Word. If you're meeting with a group, the leader will again keep track of time. At the end of two minutes, you may share with the group what came to you in the silence if you wish.*

14. *If you're meeting with a group, how can the members pray for you? If you're using this study on your own, what would you like to say to God right now?*

LIVE IT

This week, each reading will focus on the theme of compassion. Read each passage slowly, pausing to think about what is being said. Rather than approaching this as an assignment to complete, think of it as an opportunity to meet with the One who loves you most. Use any of the questions that are helpful.

Day 1

Read Psalm 51:1–2. For what does the psalmist need God's compassion in this passage?

Why is God's compassion especially necessary in such a situation?

_____

_____

_____

Do you need this kind of compassion today? If so, for what? If not, when have you needed it in the past?

_____

_____

_____

Thank God for His deep compassion on you as a sinner.

Day 2

Read Psalm 77:5–12. This psalm was written when the Jews were in exile after the Babylonians destroyed their nation. The psalmist is trying to make sense of the calamity that has happened to his people even though God is still God. What is hard for him to understand?

_____

_____

_____

What does he do in order to refocus on what he knows about God?

_____

_____

_____

Has anything happened to you that you have trouble understanding in light of who God is? If so, what is your struggle?

To sustain your trust in God's compassion, remind yourself today of what God has done for you and for His people in the past.

Day 3

Read Psalm 111:4–5. Sometimes, a word that is translated as "compassionate" in one version of the Bible is translated as "merciful" in another. How are mercy and compassion related?

Have you ever thought about the food you eat as an evidence of God's compassion? How is this significant to you?

What other evidences of God's compassion have you seen in the past day?

_____

_____

_____

Look for more examples of God's compassion as you go through this day.

Day 4

Read Psalm 116:3–9. How did the psalmist experience God's compassion?

_____

_____

_____

Do you ever feel "overcome by distress and sorrow" (verse 3)? How could the rest of this passage help believers in Christ when they feel that way?

_____

_____

_____

What if the Lord doesn't make your suffering go away? Can you still say that He is good to you? Why did you answer the way you did?

_____

_____

_____

Today, remind yourself of a time when God came through for you. Let this encourage you as you go through whatever you're facing.

Day 5

Read Isaiah 49:14–16. What do you think would move a person to say, "The LORD has forsaken me" (verse 14)?

_____

_____

_____

_____

How does this passage comfort a son or daughter of God who feels forgotten?

_____

_____

_____

_____

In what aspect of your current life does is it help you to know that the Lord has engraved His children on the palms of His hands (see verse 16)?

_____

_____

_____

_____

Thank God today that He will never, ever, forget those who surrender their lives to Him.

HEALING LOVE

CONSIDER IT

It's easy to talk about God's love, but we all want to see it demonstrated. Among the most powerful ways He communicates His love to us is by an act of healing. Healing touches the core of our longings—we long to be well and whole, free from suffering, and able to live the way we were designed to live. During Jesus' earthly ministry, He spent much of His time healing the sick to demonstrate that He had the power and the compassion of God.

While we can't expect total and permanent healing in this lifetime, Jesus still wants to heal us in some manner in our lives. He cares about the disease in our souls as well as in our bodies. He wants us to persevere in seeking Him, because in Him is the power and compassion we yearn for.

In this session, we will look at two stories of Jesus healing people to see how they reflect His eagerness to work in the lives of His followers. We will also reflect on the soul healing that He is even more eager to give anyone who will turn to Him.

1. *If you could ask Jesus to heal one thing for you or for someone else, what would it be?*

_____

_____

_____

2. *Have you or someone you know ever received a healing that you asked God for? If so, briefly tell about that experience.*

_____

_____

_____

EXPERIENCE IT

Many people are selective about which parts of themselves they bring to Me in prayer. Some hesitate to approach Me about traits they consider shameful or embarrassing. Others are so used to living with painful feelings—loneliness, fear, guilt, shame—that it never occurs to them to ask for help in dealing with those things. Still others get so preoccupied with their struggles that they forget I'm even here. This is not My way for you, beloved.

There are hurting parts of you that I desire to heal. Some of them have been with you so long that you consider them facets of your identity. You carry them with you wherever you go, barely aware of their impact on your life. I want to help you learn to walk in freedom. However, you are so addicted to certain painful patterns that it will take time to break free from them. Only repeatedly exposing them to My loving Presence will bring you long-term healing. As you grow increasingly free, you'll be released to experience My Joy in greater and greater measure!

—FROM *JESUS ALWAYS*, OCTOBER 28

3. *Can you identify with being selective about what you take to God in prayer? If so, why do you suppose you do that?*

_____

_____

_____

4. *What are some ways you could train yourself to repeatedly expose your broken areas to Jesus' loving presence?*

_____

_____

_____

I want you to trust Me enough to relax and enjoy My Presence. I did not design you to live in a state of hyper-vigilance—feeling and acting as if you are constantly in the midst of an emergency. Your body is wonderfully crafted to "gear up" when necessary and then to "gear down" when the crisis is over. But because you live in such a broken world, you find it difficult to let down your guard and relax. I want you to remember that I am with you all the time and that I am totally worthy of your confidence. *Pour out your heart to Me*, committing all the things that are troubling you into My sovereign care.

The more you *lean on Me*, the more fully you can enjoy My Presence. As you relax in My healing Light, I shine Peace into your mind and heart. Your awareness of My Presence with you grows stronger, and *My unfailing Love* soaks into your inner being. *Trust in Me*, beloved, *with all your heart and mind*.

—From *Jesus Always*, December 4

5. *How easy is it for you to lean on Jesus, let down your guard, and relax? What helps you? What gets in the way?*

_____

_____

_____

_____

6. *Light is a common biblical metaphor for Jesus' powerful presence. Why is light a fitting symbol of Jesus? What is it about His presence that is like light?*

_____

_____

_____

_____

STUDY IT

Read aloud the following passages from Mark 1:40–42 and 5:24–34 in the *English Standard Version*. These verses relate two encounters between Jesus and sick people. As you read, note that leprosy wasn't just any illness—it was contagious and symbolized sin. Therefore, any person who touched a leper was considered unclean and had to go through a series of rituals (offering a sacrifice and washing) to be considered clean again. Likewise, bleeding made a person unclean, and so a normal rabbi would have been furious to be touched not just by a woman (that was bad enough in ancient culture) but by a bleeding woman who made him unclean. However, Jesus' attitude was that unclean people couldn't make Him unclean. Rather, He made them clean and healed them.

> 1:40 And a leper came to [Jesus], imploring him, and kneeling said to him, "If you will, you can make me clean." 41 Moved with pity, he stretched out his hand and touched him and said to him, "I will; be clean." 42 And immediately the leprosy left him, and he was made clean.

> 5:24 And a great crowd followed him and thronged about him. 25 And there was a woman who had had a discharge of blood for twelve years, 26 and who had suffered much under many physicians, and had spent all that she had, and was no better but rather grew worse. 27 She had heard the reports about Jesus and came up behind him in the crowd and touched his garment. 28 For she said, "If I touch even his garments, I will be made well." 29 And immediately the flow of blood dried up, and she felt in her body that she was healed of her disease. 30 And Jesus, perceiving in himself that power had gone out from him, immediately turned about in the crowd and said, "Who touched my garments?" 31 And his disciples said to him, "You see the crowd pressing around you, and yet you say, 'Who touched me?'" 32 And he looked around to see who had done it. 33 But the woman, knowing what had happened to her, came in fear and trembling and fell down before him and told him the whole truth. 34 And he said to her, "Daughter, your faith has made you well; go in peace, and be healed of your disease."

7. *How does the first passage show that Jesus loved the leper? How does the second passage reveal that He loved the bleeding woman?*

_____

_____

_____

_____

8. *What might have made each of these people—the leper and the woman—hesitate before going to Jesus for His healing love?*

_____

_____

_____

_____

9. *If God loves everyone, why do you suppose He doesn't heal everyone who asks?*

_____

_____

_____

_____

10. *Why do you think Jesus wanted the woman to identify herself and not just be healed anonymously?*

_____

_____

_____

11. *How do these stories about Jesus healing people affect you? Are you drawn closer to Him, or do you find yourself thinking about healings you haven't received?*

12. *Take two minutes of silence to reread the passages, looking for a sentence, phrase, or even one word that stands out as something Jesus may want you to focus on in your life. If you're meeting with a group, the leader will keep track of time. At the end of two minutes, you may share with the group the word or phrase that came to you in the silence.*

13. *Read the passages aloud again. Take another two minutes of silence, prayerfully considering what response God might want you to make to what you have read in His Word. If you're meeting with a group, the leader will again keep track of time. At the end of two minutes, you may share with the group what came to you in the silence if you wish.*

14. *If you're meeting with a group, how can the members pray for you? If you're using this study on your own, what would you like to say to God right now?*

_____

_____

_____

LIVE IT

This week's readings will focus on Jesus' acts of love. Read each passage slowly, pausing to think about what is being said. Rather than approaching this as an assignment to complete, think of it as an opportunity to meet with the One who loves you most. Use any of the questions that are helpful.

Day 1

Read Luke 7:11–17. What are the signs of Jesus' love in this story?

_____

_____

_____

_____

Jesus didn't raise many people from the dead. What apparently moved him in this case?

_____

_____

_____

_____

What difference does it make to you that Jesus is Lord even over death?

Go to Jesus with your need today. Don't hesitate.

Day 2

Read Luke 8:26–39. How does Jesus demonstrate His love in this story?

Why do you think the local people responded to His loving action with fear (see verses 35, 37)?

How did the healed man respond to what Jesus had done (see verse 39)? Why was that an appropriate response to Jesus' love?

Today, tell someone something that Jesus has done for you.

Day 3

Read Mark 6:30–34. How does Jesus show His love for His disciples and for the crowd?

_____

_____

_____

What does it mean to be "like sheep without a shepherd" (verse 34)?

_____

_____

_____

How do you need a shepherd? What do you need a shepherd to do?

_____

_____

_____

Entrust yourself to Jesus' compassion. Put into His hands whatever need you have today.

Day 4

Read Luke 9:37–45. How does Jesus demonstrate His love in this story?

_____

_____

_____

Is Jesus frustrated with the man, His own disciples, or both? Does He seem less loving to you when He gets frustrated like this? Why or why not?

Why do you suppose the disciples could understand Jesus' miraculous healings but not the foretelling of His eventual betrayal (see verses 44–45)?

Go to Jesus with your needs today, but also be willing to listen if He offers you correction or instruction.

Day 5

Read Luke 19:1–10. How does Jesus demonstrate His love in this story?

How does Jesus' love change Zacchaeus' life?

If you had been present, do you think you would have shared the people's view of Jesus in verse 7? How comfortable are you with reaching out to "notorious" sinners?

_____

_____

_____

Today, ask Jesus to help you follow His example of showing love to others.

ROOTED IN LOVE

CONSIDER IT

Healthy tree roots need water and oxygen, but these elements will accomplish little if the quality of the soil is poor. Roots need soil that is loose enough for them to penetrate and for water to drain away. Hardpan (heavily compacted soil) doesn't let roots pierce it and doesn't allow rainwater to drain away. The result is shallow roots that are either too dry or sitting in water.

Humans are like trees in that we need strong roots—only ours are spiritual roots. Our souls need soil that nourishes us and into which we can sink our roots. Love is that nourishing soil—not the hard-packed circumstances the world throws at us, but the loose, rich soil of God's love. The irony is that while this rich soil is readily available to anyone who seeks it, so many people resist rooting themselves in it. They doubt that it exists—or that it exists for them.

But it is available for each and every one of us. In this session, we will investigate what we can do, and what God does do, to root us in the love that will make us grow and flourish.

1. *How would you describe the home environment in which you grew up? Did you feel loved? Were you well cared for?*

2. *How do you think your experience as a child has affected the way you experience God's love?*

Experience It

My Love will never let you go! It has an eternal grip on you. You live in a world that is unpredictable and unsafe in many ways. As you look around, you see landscape littered with broken promises.

However, My Love is a promise that will never be broken. *Though the mountains be shaken and the hills be removed, yet My unfailing Love for you will not be shaken.* The prophet Isaiah is painting a picture of dire circumstances: quaking mountains and disappearing hills. No matter *what* is happening, My Love is unshakable. You can build your life on it!

Sometimes My children believe I care for them but still find it difficult to receive My Love in full measure. I want you to learn *to grasp how wide and long and high and deep is My Love for you.* Ask My Spirit to empower you *to know this Love that surpasses knowledge.* Break free from faulty self-images so you can view yourself as I see you—radiant in *My righteousness*, wrapped in luminous Love.

—From *Jesus Always*, February 8

3. *Have the broken promises of friends and family in your life affected your inclination to trust God's love? If so, what's the solution to that?*

_____

_____

_____

4. *What is the danger in viewing ourselves differently than God sees us? How can we learn His perspective of us?*

_____

_____

_____

I want you to know the depth and breadth of *My Love that surpasses knowledge*. There is an enormous difference between knowing Me and knowing *about* Me. Similarly, experiencing My loving Presence is vastly different from knowing facts about My character. To experience My Presence, you need the empowering work of My Spirit. Ask Him to *strengthen you with Power in your inner being* so that you can *know My Love* in full measure.

Since the moment of your salvation, I have been alive in your heart. The more room you make for Me there, the more I can fill you with My Love. There are several ways to expand this space in your heart. It's crucial to take time with Me—enjoying My Presence and studying My Word. It is also vital to stay in communication with Me. As the apostle Paul wrote, *pray continually*. This joyful practice will keep you close to Me. Finally, let My Love flow through you to others—in both your words and your actions. This *makes My Love in you complete*.

—FROM *JESUS ALWAYS*, MAY 22

5. *How would you describe the difference between knowing God and knowing about God?*

6. *How have you been doing the past few weeks in taking time to be with God each day? How has that affected you?*

Study It

Read aloud the following passage from Ephesians 3:14–21, in which the apostle Paul offers a prayer for his fellow Christians in the city of Ephesus. As you read, note that in verses 14 and 15, the Greek words translated "Father" and "family" come from the same root. We may have had flawed parents who didn't adequately love us, but God, our heavenly Father, is the true model of familial love. Also, in the Greek it's clear that Paul primarily prays for the believers to be empowered through the Holy Spirit so that several things may happen: (1) Christ may dwell in their hearts, (2) they will be rooted and established in His love, (3) they may have the power to grasp the extent of that love, and (4) they may be filled with God's fullness. Wrapping our minds around God's love requires the presence of God's Spirit in our lives.

> [14] For this reason I kneel before the Father, [15] from whom every family in heaven and on earth derives its name. [16] I pray that out of his glorious riches he may strengthen you with power through his Spirit in your inner being, [17] so that Christ may dwell in your hearts through faith. And I pray that you, being rooted and established in love, [18] may have power, together with all the Lord's holy people, to grasp how wide and long and high and deep is the love of Christ, [19] and to know this love that surpasses knowledge—that you may be filled to the measure of all the fullness of God.
>
> [20] Now to him who is able to do immeasurably more than all we ask or imagine, according to his power that is at work within us, [21] to him be glory in the church and in Christ Jesus throughout all generations, for ever and ever! Amen.

7. *What do you think it means for believers in Christ to be rooted in God's love (see verse 17)?*

_____

_____

_____

8. *What would be the evidence in a believer's life that he or she is rooted and established in God's love?*

9. *According to verse 16, one of the keys to being rooted in God's love is to be strengthened with power by God's Spirit in your inner being. The Holy Spirit makes rootedness possible. Do you need to be strengthened by God's Spirit? Or is that already part of your day-to-day life?*

10. *What do you think it means to know God's love that surpasses knowledge (see verse 19)?*

11. *What does Paul say about God's power in verse 20? How is that helpful for you?*

12. *Take two minutes of silence to reread the passage, looking for a sentence, phrase, or even one word that stands out as something Jesus may want you to focus on in your life. If you're meeting with a group, the leader will keep track of time. At the end of two minutes, you may share with the group the word or phrase that came to you in the silence.*

---

13. *Read the passage aloud again. Take another two minutes of silence, prayerfully considering what response God might want you to make to what you have read in His Word. If you're meeting with a group, the leader will again keep track of time. At the end of two minutes, you may share with the group what came to you in the silence if you wish.*

---

14. *If you're meeting with a group, how can the members pray for you? If you're using this study on your own, what would you like to say to God right now?*

LIVE IT

This week's readings will focus on additional items that Paul states about God's love in Romans, Ephesians, and Philippians. Read each passage slowly, pausing to think about what is being said. Rather than approaching this as an assignment to complete, think of it as an opportunity to meet with the One who loves you most. Use any of the questions that are helpful.

Day 1

Read Ephesians 1:4–6. What does this passage say about what God has done for His children in love?

How would you restate this passage in your own words?

Why should your gratitude be overflowing for this evidence of God's love if you are His child?

Today, look for a practical way to live out your gratitude to God.

Day 2

Read Ephesians 5:8–14. What does this passage say God has done for His children out of love?

_____

_____

_____

What does it mean to "walk as children of light" (verse 8)?

_____

_____

_____

How does Paul say that Christians are to respond to this act of love from God?

_____

_____

_____

Today, look for a chance to love someone else with the same kind of generous and merciful love that God has offered to you.

Day 3

Read Ephesians 5:15–21. What does it mean to "walk circumspectly" (verse 15 KJV)?

_____

_____

_____

How do you see the wisdom that God provides to His children as an act of His love?

_____

_____

_____

_____

How does Paul say that you are to respond to this gift of love from God?

_____

_____

_____

_____

Today, seize the chance to share God's wisdom and love with others who may not know Him.

Day 4

Read Romans 12:9–16. What does Paul say God's love looks like in the life of a believer?

_____

_____

_____

_____

How easy or hard is it for you to exhibit this kind of love? Explain.

What does it mean to be "wise in your own opinion" (verse 16)? How can this lead to ignoring what is necessary to truly love others with God's love?

Spend some time today reflecting on the kind of love that God has shown to His children and how He expects you to demonstrate that love to others.

Day 5

Read Philippians 2:1–4. In verse 1, Paul says, "If you have any . . . comfort from [Christ's] love." Do you have any comfort from Christ's love? If so, describe how you are comforted by it.

How does Paul want God's children to respond to the comfort they have received from Christ's love (see verse 2)?

_____

_____

_____

_____

How does Paul describe Christlike love in verses 3–4?

_____

_____

_____

_____

Look for a chance to pass along Jesus' kind of love today.

FEARLESS LOVE

CONSIDER IT

Nothing can separate believers in Christ from God's love. His love is ever-lasting and abounding, compassionate and healing. We need to live rooted in the awareness of that love no matter what happens to us. If we do live rooted, something begins to happen in us. We develop a love for God and others that is fearless. We are no longer driven by the fear that we won't be loved enough if we make mistakes or have committed sins. We are secure, so we can turn our gaze to the magnificence of God and the needs of others.

In the "Live It" studies you have gone through on your own each week, you have already seen that the apostle Paul asks believers in Christ to treat others with the same kind of love they have received from God. In this session, we'll look at how the apostle John sees the love we receive from God and the love we give to others. When we understand how intertwined they are, it only makes sense to give away what we have been given.

Fearless love is bold, confident, and generous. It doesn't shrink from the weight of others' needs. In fact, it delights in the ability to carry some of that weight with God's mighty strength. Embracing Jesus' love takes us on a journey outward, from self-focus to a joyful focus on others.

1. *Some people seem to be born more naturally fearful than others. When you were a child, were you more likely to be fearful in a new situation, or fearless? Give an example.*

_____

_____

_____

2. *What about now? Do you tend to be a risk taker or a risk avoider? Does that quality work well for you or tend to get in your way?*

_____

_____

_____

EXPERIENCE IT

You love Me because I first loved you. I had My eye on you long before you were interested in Me. I noticed everything about you and followed you everywhere. I orchestrated circumstances and events in your life to help you see your need of Me. I provided people and teaching that told you the truth about Me in ways you could understand. My Spirit worked within you to make you spiritually alive—enabling you to *receive Me and believe in My Name.* All of this flowed out of My deep, powerful affection for you. *I have loved you with an everlasting Love!*

The more you realize the immensity of My ardor for you, the more fully you can love *Me.* This enables you to grow, little by little, into the person I designed you to be. As you spend time in My tender Presence, it becomes easier for you to delight in Me and to show kindness to other people. When you are with others, ask Me to help you love them—with *My* Love.

—FROM *JESUS ALWAYS,* APRIL 19

3. *When God called Jeremiah to be a prophet for His people, he said, "Before I formed you in the womb I knew you, before you were born I set you apart" (Jeremiah 1:5). What are some ways that God knew you and revealed His love for you long before you were even aware of Him?*

4. *Why is it important to contemplate the many ways God has shown His love for us?*

Do not let fear of mistakes immobilize you or make you anxious. In this life you *will* err sometimes because you're only human, with limited knowledge and understanding. When you're facing a major decision, learn as much as you can about the matter. *Seek My Face*—and My help. I will *guide you with My counsel* as you think things out in My Presence. When the time is right, go ahead and make the decision, even though the outcome is uncertain. Pray for My will to be done in this matter, and release the results to Me.

Fear has to do with punishment. If you have been punished unjustly or severely mistreated, it is natural for you to dread making mistakes. When choices need to be made, anxiety can cloud your thinking—perhaps even immobilizing you. The remedy is to remember that *I am with you* and for you—that you don't have to perform well for Me to keep loving you. Absolutely nothing, including your worst mistakes, *can separate you from My Love*!

—FROM *JESUS ALWAYS*, OCTOBER 4

5. *How can embracing Jesus' love help lessen your fear of making mistakes?*

_____

_____

_____

_____

6. *How do you typically respond when you make a mistake? Are you hard on yourself? Do you find that you can keep the mistake in proper perspective and move forward? What makes the difference for you?*

_____

_____

_____

_____

STUDY IT

Read aloud the following passages from 1 John 4:7–12 and 15–21. As you do, note that the apostle John wrote this letter (probably to churches in the city of Ephesus) to address divisions that were tearing the churches apart. Doctrinal disagreements were heated, and John wanted the believers to know which leaders and members they could trust. One standard he held up was correct doctrine about who Jesus really was. But correct doctrine alone was not enough—another essential hallmark of a true follower of Jesus was whether he or she exhibited love that mirrored Jesus' kind of love. In this excerpt from his letter, John explains why fearless, unselfish love stands alongside right doctrine as a mark of real faith.

[7] Dear friends, let us love one another, for love comes from God. Everyone who loves has been born of God and knows God. [8] Whoever does not love does not know God, because God is love. [9] This is how God showed his love among us: He sent his one and only Son into the world that we might live through him. [10] This is love: not that we loved God, but that he loved us and sent his Son as an atoning sacrifice for our sins. [11] Dear friends, since God so loved us, we also ought to love one another. [12] No one has ever seen God; but if we love one another, God lives in us and his love is made complete in us . . .

[15] If anyone acknowledges that Jesus is the Son of God, God lives in them and they in God. [16] And so we know and rely on the love God has for us.

God is love. Whoever lives in love lives in God, and God in them. [17] This is how love is made complete among us so that we will have confidence on the day of judgment: In this world we are like Jesus. [18] There is no fear in love. But perfect love drives out fear, because fear has to do with punishment. The one who fears is not made perfect in love.

[19] We love because he first loved us. [20] Whoever claims to love God yet hates a brother or sister is a liar. For whoever does not love their

brother and sister, whom they have seen, cannot love God, whom they have not seen. [21] And he has given us this command: Anyone who loves God must also love their brother and sister.

7. *Describe in your own words what is meant by the statement "God is love" (verse 8).*

_____

_____

_____

_____

8. *What is the standard of love that John provides in verses 9–10? How is this different from mere strong emotions?*

_____

_____

_____

_____

9. *For followers of Christ, how is loving one another related to experiencing the love that God has freely provided to them (see verses 7–12)?*

_____

_____

_____

_____

10. *God's love is made complete in His sons and daughters not by experiencing it but by giving it away to others (see verse 12). How is this significant for you?*

11. *According to verse 18, the key to living without fear of God's judgment is to concentrate on loving Him and loving others. Living a lifestyle of love drives out fear. Have you experienced that to be the case? If so, describe your experience.*

12. *Take two minutes of silence to reread the passage, looking for a sentence, phrase, or even one word that stands out as something Jesus may want you to focus on in your life. If you're meeting with a group, the leader will keep track of time. At the end of two minutes, you may share with the group the word or phrase that came to you in the silence.*

13. *Read the passage aloud again. Take another two minutes of silence, prayerfully considering what response God might want you to make to what you have read in His Word. If you're meeting with a group, the leader will again keep track of time. At the end of two minutes, you may share with the group what came to you in the silence if you wish.*

14. *If you're meeting with a group, how can the members pray for you? If you're using this study on your own, what would you like to say to God right now?*

LIVE IT

This week's readings will continue to focus on the topic of love as seen in the writings of the apostle John. Read each passage slowly, pausing to think about what is being said. Rather than approaching this as an assignment to complete, think of it as an opportunity to meet with the One who loves you most. Use any of the questions that are helpful.

Day 1

Read John 3:16–18. What is the rock-solid, foundational reason we have for knowing that God loves us?

_____

_____

_____

_____

Judging by this passage and your current relationship with God, does He condemn you? How do you know?

_____

_____

_____

_____

These are elementary truths of the faith. Why is it worthwhile to remind ourselves about them?

_____

_____

_____

_____

Make a note to remind yourself of God's love for you throughout this day.

Day 2

Read John 13:1–10. According to verses 1 and 3, what did Jesus know that motivated Him to express His love for the disciples in such a humble way?

_____

_____

_____

_____

How did Peter react when Jesus tried to wash his feet (see verses 6–8)? What did Jesus mean when He said that unless He washed Peter's feet, Peter would have no part with Him?

_____

_____

_____

In the culture of the day, washing dirty feet was the job of the lowest slave. What would be an act of love like that in our society?

_____

_____

_____

_____

Be on the lookout for a way to "wash someone's feet" today.

Day 3

Read John 13:34–35. What reasons for loving one another does Jesus give in this passage? Why are these reasons important?

Jesus says His followers must love the way He has loved them. How has He loved us?

When have you had an opportunity to love someone with Jesus' kind of love during the past week?

Look for a chance to love someone with the love that Jesus has modeled for you.

Day 4

Read John 14:23–24. What connection between love and obedience does Jesus describe in these verses?

How comfortable are you with Jesus' expectation that you will obey Him if you are part of God's family? Is "obedience" a negative word? Why did you answer the way you did?

Yesterday, we saw that the teaching Jesus wants us to obey is about loving one another. Does it make sense that Jesus says anyone who loves Him will love His people? Why or why not?

Today, talk with God about obedience, telling Him honestly how you relate to that word.

Day 5

Read 1 John 3:16–18. How does John define love in this passage?

_____

_____

_____

_____

What reason does John give for being generous with your material possessions?

_____

_____

_____

_____

What is your policy about giving your material possessions to believers in need?

_____

_____

_____

_____

Today, pay attention to the material needs of Christians nearby you or in poor countries. Look for a way to be helpful.

PERSEVERING LOVE

CONSIDER IT

Think of someone who is hard for you to love. A wayward teen. A critical parent. A withdrawn spouse. A friend who has gossiped about you. A boss who makes unreasonable demands. This person makes your life difficult and doesn't treat you with love. Feelings of hurt, disappointment, and even anger are likely to well up when you think about this individual.

Now consider this is exactly the way you were—or are—in the way you treat God, and God has loved you anyway. He has never given up on you, no matter how unfaithful you might have been. Maybe you have gone days or weeks without praying, and He has not hardened His heart toward you. Maybe you have done things you don't want to tell your Christian friends about, and still, God has stuck with you. He welcomes you back every time.

In this session, we will consider love that perseveres in spite of obstacles and hurts. We will look at God's persevering love and the ways He asks us to imitate Him—how He asks us to seek the highest good of another person no matter what. So, as you go through this session, keep that hard-to-love person in mind—and consider whether God is standing ready to empower you with persevering love for that individual.

1. *What were you like when you were a teenager? Were you typically challenging and hard to love, or did you tend to be more compliant and easygoing?*

_____

_____

_____

2. *How often do you get impatient? Under what circumstances?*

_____

_____

_____

EXPERIENCE IT

You are fully known. I know absolutely everything about you, and I love you with perfect, *unfailing Love.* Many people are searching for greater self-understanding and self-acceptance. Underlying their search is a desire to find someone who truly understands them and accepts them as they are. I am the Someone who can fully satisfy this deep-seated longing. It is in your relationship with Me that you discover who you really are.

I encourage you to be real with Me—dropping all pretenses and opening yourself fully to Me. As you draw near, utter these inspired words: *"Search me, O God, and know my heart; test me, and know my anxious thoughts."* In the Light of My holy gaze, you will see things you need to change. But don't despair; I will help you. Continue resting in My Presence, receiving My Love that flows freely into you through your openness to Me. Take time to let this powerful Love soak in deeply—filling up your empty spaces and overflowing into joyous worship. Rejoice greatly, for you are fully known and forever loved!

—FROM *JESUS ALWAYS,* JANUARY 14

3. *What can you do to drop all pretenses and open yourself fully to Christ?*

---

4. *In Psalm 139:1, David writes, "O LORD, You have searched me and known me" (ESV). God knows everything about you—and still loves you. How do you reconcile the assurance that God loves you as you are, but there are things about you that He wants to change?*

Love is patient. Notice that the very first adjective the apostle Paul uses to describe love is "patient." I treasure this quality in My followers, even though it is not highly visible in most twenty-first-century depictions of love. Patient people can stay calm while enduring lengthy waits or dealing with difficult people and problems. I encourage you to examine your own life: to see how you respond to waiting and difficulties. This will give you a good measure of how patient—how loving—you are.

"Patience" is listed fourth in *the fruit of the Spirit*. My Spirit will help you grow in this important character trait, especially as you ask Him. Some Christians are afraid to pray for patience. They fear that I'll answer their prayer by subjecting them to severe suffering and trials. However, suffering serves an important purpose in My kingdom, and trials are not optional. They *come so that your faith may be proved genuine and may result in praise, glory, and honor* to Me!

—From *Jesus Always*, June 14

5. *What helps you to be patient toward others? What tends to get in the way?*

_____

_____

_____

_____

6. *How do trials help you grow in patience? What other benefits do they provide if you let them?*

_____

_____

_____

_____

STUDY IT

Read aloud the following passages from 1 Corinthians 13:4–8 and 12–13. In these verses, Paul describes what the Bible means by loving others. It's a high standard, yet it is the way Jesus loved people during His time on earth, and it is the way He continues to love us today. As you read, note that in the original context of this passage, Paul was correcting a wrong attitude among the believers in Corinth. They were assigning prestige to the flashier spiritual gifts, such as prophecy and speaking in tongues, and were guilty of pride, self-serving attitudes, anger, and other qualities that were unloving. Paul's description of love here is meant to be an antidote to the poisonous attitudes the Corinthians were exhibiting.

> [4] Love is patient, love is kind. It does not envy, it does not boast, it is not proud. [5] It does not dishonor others, it is not self-seeking, it is not easily angered, it keeps no record of wrongs. [6] Love does not delight in evil but rejoices with the truth. [7] It always protects, always trusts, always hopes, always perseveres.
>
> [8] Love never fails. . . . [12] For now we see only a reflection as in a mirror; then we shall see face to face. Now I know in part; then I shall know fully, even as I am fully known.
>
> [13] And now these three remain: faith, hope and love. But the greatest of these is love.

7. Paul says in verse 12 that believers in Christ are "fully known." How does being fully known by God help a person learn to love the way Paul describes in verses 4–8?

8. *Look again at the qualities of love described in verses 4–8. How does Jesus show that kind of love to you each day?*

_____

_____

_____

9. *To "persevere" is to continue doing something despite difficulties. Why is it important that love always perseveres?*

_____

_____

_____

10. *When Paul says that love "always trusts" (verse 7), it doesn't mean people are universally trustworthy. Jesus didn't trust everyone during His time on earth (see John 2:24.) Instead, Paul is saying we should always trust God in loving others, regardless of how untrustworthy people may be. How might this play out in a relationship with someone who isn't fully trustworthy?*

_____

_____

_____

11. *Which quality of love in verses 4–8 is hardest for you to practice consistently?*

_____

_____

_____

12. *Take two minutes of silence to reread the passage, looking for a sentence, phrase, or even one word that stands out as something Jesus may want you to focus on in your life. If you're meeting with a group, the leader will keep track of time. At the end of two minutes, you may share with the group the word or phrase that came to you in the silence.*

13. *Read the passage aloud again. Take another two minutes of silence, prayerfully considering what response God might want you to make to what you have read in His Word. If you're meeting with a group, the leader will again keep track of time. At the end of two minutes, you may share with the group what came to you in the silence if you wish.*

14. *If you're meeting with a group, how can the members pray for you? If you're using this study on your own, what would you like to say to God right now?*

LIVE IT

This week's readings will focus on the benefits of perseverance when it comes to loving one another. Read each passage slowly, pausing to think about what is being said. Rather than approaching this as an assignment to complete, think of it as an opportunity to meet with the One who loves you most. Use any of the questions that are helpful.

Day 1

Read Luke 8:4–15. In verse 15, Jesus says, "The seed on good soil stands for those with a noble and good heart, who hear the word, retain it, and by persevering produce a crop." Why do you suppose perseverance (or patience) is so important in producing a crop in a Christian's life?

What do you think is the crop (or fruit) that your life is supposed to produce?

How hard is it for you to persevere at something difficult? Why is that the case?

Ask God to show you where you need to persevere today in order to show His love to others.

Day 2

Read Romans 5:3–5. In this passage, Paul says suffering ideally produces perseverance—yet we know that suffering can produce bitterness and hopelessness instead. What do you think has to happen in your attitude in order for suffering to produce God's intended result?

_____

_____

_____

_____

How has suffering affected you? How has it affected your attitude in dealing with difficulties?

_____

_____

_____

_____

What benefits of perseverance does Paul name in verses 3 and 4? How valuable are those to you? Why did you answer the way you did?

_____

_____

_____

_____

Look for ways to respond to life with perseverance instead of bitterness.

Day 3

Read Hebrews 10:36–39. According to verse 36, for what reason do you need perseverance?

_____

_____

_____

_____

What is the promise given to believers in Christ for enduring in their faith?

_____

_____

_____

_____

Is it hard for you to persevere in doing the will of God? What would help you?

_____

_____

_____

_____

If you are committed to Christ, remind yourself today that you are one of those who has faith and sticks with what God has given you to do.

Day 4

Read Hebrews 12:1–3. The "great cloud of witnesses" described in verse 1 are the faithful people of the Old Testament who set an example of persevering faith. Can you think of one witness in the Old or New Testament—or someone who has lived since then—who has set a good example for you in demonstrating persevering love?

The writer of this passage encourages us to "run with perseverance the race marked out for us, fixing our eyes on Jesus" (verses 1–2). How does focusing on Jesus' love and what He has done for you motivate you to persevere more today (see verses 2–3)?

What was "the joy" set before Jesus (verse 2)? What is the joy set before you that can motivate you to persevere?

If you're tempted to lose heart today, refocus your mind on the joy set before you.

Day 5

Read James 1:2–4. What does perseverance produce in followers of Christ (see verse 4)?

Have you experienced the testing of your faith producing perseverance? If so, when?

How badly do you want to be "mature and complete" (verse 4)? Be honest with yourself about this. Why did you answer the way you did?

Today, look for ways God might be using the trials you face to produce maturity and enduring faith within you.

LEADER'S NOTES

Thank you for your willingness to lead a group through this *Jesus Always* study. The rewards of leading are different from the rewards of participating, and we hope you find your own walk with Jesus deepened by this experience. In many ways, your group meeting will be structured like other Bible studies in which you've participated. You'll want to open in prayer, for example, and ask people to silence their phones. These leader's notes will focus on elements of the study that may be new to you.

CONSIDER IT

This first portion of the study functions as an icebreaker. It gets the group members thinking about the topic at hand by asking them to share from their own experience. Some people may be tempted to tell a long story in response to one of these questions, but the goal is to keep the answers brief. Ideally, you want everyone in the group to have a chance to answer the *Consider It* questions, so you may want to say up front that everyone needs to limit his or her answer to one minute.

With the rest of the study, it is generally not a good idea to go around the circle and have everyone answer every question—a free-flowing discussion is more desirable. But with the *Consider It* questions, you can go around the circle. Encourage shy people to share, but don't force them. Tell the group they should feel free to pass if they prefer not to answer a question.

EXPERIENCE IT

This is the group's chance to talk about excerpts from the *Jesus Always* devotional. You will need to monitor this discussion closely so that you have enough time for the actual study of God's Word that follows. If the group has a long and rich discussion on one of the devotional excerpts, you may choose to skip the other one and move on to the Bible study. Don't feel obliged to cover every *Experience It* question if the conversation is fruitful. On the other hand, do move on if the group gets off on a tangent.

STUDY IT

Try to do the *Study It* exercise in session 1 on your own before the group meets the first time so you can coach people on what to expect. Note that this section may be a little different from Bible studies your group has done in the past. The group will talk about the Bible passage as usual, but then there will be several minutes of silence so individuals can pray about what God might want to say to them personally through the reading. It will be up to you to keep track of the time and call people back to the discussion when the time is up. (There are some good timer apps that play a gentle chime or other pleasant sound instead of a disruptive noise.) If members aren't used to being silent in a group, brief them on what to expect.

Don't be afraid to let people sit in silence. Two minutes of quiet may seem like a long time at first, but it will help to train group members to sit in silence with God when they are alone. They can remain where they are in the circle, or if you have space, you can let them go off by themselves to other rooms at your instruction. If your group meets in a home, ask the host before the meeting which rooms are available for use. Some people will be more comfortable in the quiet if they have a bit of space from others.

When the group reconvenes after the time of silence, invite them to share what they experienced. There are several questions provided in this study guide that you can ask. Note that it's not necessary to cover every question if the group has a good discussion going. It's also not necessary to go around the circle and make everyone share.

Don't be concerned if the group members are reserved and slow to share after the exercise. People are often quiet when they are pulling together their ideas, and the exercise will have been a new experience for many of them. Just ask a question and let it hang in the air until someone speaks up. You can then say, "Thank you. What about others? What came to you when you sat with the passage?"

Some people may say they found it hard to quiet their minds enough to focus on the passage for those few minutes. Tell them this is okay. They are practicing a skill, and sometimes skills take time to learn. If they learn to sit quietly with God's Word in a group, they will become much more comfortable sitting with the Word on their own. Remind them that spending time in the Bible each day is one of the most valuable things they can do as believers in Christ.

PREPARATION

It's not necessary for group members to prepare anything for the study ahead of time. However, at the end of each study are five days' worth of suggestions for spending time in God's Word during the next week. These daily times are optional but valuable, so encourage the group to do them. Also, invite them to bring their questions and insights to the group at your next meeting, especially if they had a breakthrough moment or if they didn't understand something.

As the leader, there are a few things you should do to prepare for each meeting:

- *Read through the session.* This will help you become familiar with the content and know how to structure the discussion times.

- *Spend five to ten minutes doing the* Study It *questions on your own.* When the group meets, you'll be watching the clock, so you'll probably have a more fulfilling time with the passage if you do the exercise ahead of time. You can then spend time in the passage again with the group. This way, you'll be sure to have the key verses for that session deeply in your mind.

- *Pray for your group.* Pray especially that God will guide them in how to embrace the love that Jesus has demonstrated for them and, in turn, share that love with others in their world who need to experience it.

- *Bring extra supplies to your meeting.* Group members should bring their own pens for writing notes on the Bible reflection, but it is a good idea to have extras available for those who forget. You may also want to bring paper and Bibles for those who may have neglected to bring their study guides to the meeting.

Below you will find suggested answers for some of the study questions. Note that in many cases there is no one right answer, especially when the group members are sharing their personal experiences.

Session 1: Inseparable Love

1. *Answers will vary. For some, the childhood losses may be of pets, but for others it could be a best friend or even a parent, which are certainly more difficult to accept. It's appropriate to say something like, "I'm so sorry that happened to you," or, "That had to be very hard," when a significant loss is named.*

2. *Give people time to think about this. Some will know immediately how they have been affected, but others will not. With the loss of a pet, for example, there may not be much effect in the present—it's the major losses that leave their marks. In some cases, the impact of a major loss will be a decision not to attach too much to anything or anyone. Be sensitive as you explore and discuss this question with the group.*

3. *God says in His Word that nothing will separate us from His love. It's a promise for those who belong to Him—and He does not lie. Beyond that, experiencing His permanent presence as we walk through life and endure suffering gradually teaches us that He is dependable. Having godly, dependable people in our lives can also encourage our faith.*

4. *If it's not easy to cling to Jesus with confidence, it could be evidence that we aren't securely convinced that nothing can separate us from His love. Our earthly separations from people or things we've loved have taught us not to trust. We need to be honest with Jesus about this so that we can grow in this area.*

5. *Let those who have stories about receiving God's comfort encourage those who need that same comfort. Those who haven't been in the habit of spending time in God's presence (or who don't yet know Him) will have a harder time coming up with an answer—but that in itself will be instructive. Also, some may have stories of receiving God's comfort through another person. That counts! God often works through people.*

6. *Offering comfort to another person can be as simple as listening in a way that shows empathy without giving advice or trying to fix the problem. It can also involve practical help (making a meal for someone who is recovering from surgery, for example). Distinguish comfort from advice giving, which is often not as helpful.*

7. *When Paul says God is "for" us, it means our heavenly Father is rooting for His sons and daughters. He is on our side if we are on His side! He wants what is best for us, even if that means we will suffer for a time in this life. Our Father in heaven has supplied His family on earth with all the resources necessary for a flourishing life, if we will accept His provision.*

8. *Some believers in Christ really resonate with the truth that God has declared them "not guilty" because of the death of His Son. Others may carry around feelings of guilt that were drummed into them as children. Regardless of how we feel, the "not guilty" declaration is real! But every believer needs to come to a relaxed and joyful place where they know it's true at their core. Letting people talk about their guilt feelings may help them begin to get past them.*

9. *Answers will vary. Many group members may not have thought about the fact that they tend to feel separated from God when life isn't going their way. Significant losses can make us feel that God has abandoned us. As people's feelings surface, talk about the fact that significant losses are normal in a fallen world—but they're not a sign that God has abandoned us. He grieves with His children and wants to love us in the midst of our grief.*

10. *Knowing that Jesus is interceding for His followers should encourage us because we're not on our own in dealing with our sins and the challenges of life. Jesus acts as every believer's defense attorney whenever Satan accuses him or her of wrongdoing. Jesus is also praying for His people in their need, even when they're not aware of it. Contemplating this should increase our security and reduce our anxiety.*

11. *Answers will vary. Paul's list is meant to cover all the possibilities, but each of us is unique. Trouble and hardship are probably at the top of most people's lists. Personal failings are on the list. Busyness too. Talk about how none of these things can truly separate God's children from His love—not even when they feel distant from Him—because the Bible promises He is always near them.*

12. *Answers will vary. It's fine for this process to be unfamiliar to the group at first. Be sure to keep track of time.*

13. *Answers will vary. Note that some people may find the silence intimidating at first. Their anxiety might tempt them to fill the air with noise, but it will be helpful for these group members to just take a quiet moment before God. Let them express their discomfort once you're all gathered together again, but make sure it is balanced by those who found the silence strengthening. Helping people become comfortable with this "holy quiet" will serve their private daily times with God in wonderful ways.*

14. *Take as much time as you can to pray for each other. You might have someone write down the prayer requests so you can keep track of answers to prayer.*

Session 2: Everlasting Love

1. *Answers will vary. The point here is not to blame our parents—all parents are human and thus fallible. Rather, the point is to identify a possible root of some of our difficulty in embracing God's love as being limitless and everlasting. The group members don't need to go into long stories about their parents. One minute per person should be plenty.*

2. *Often, people who felt limited love from their parents have trouble trusting that God's love is limitless. However, sometimes people who felt conditional love from their parents are overjoyed to encounter God's everlasting love and are able to exult in it. And sometimes people who received plenty of love as children don't feel a need for God as adults. So answers will vary.*

3. *God knows His children and loves them as individuals. He wants the intimacy of being on a first-name basis with them. When we belong to God, we're not just one of the crowd to Him.*

4. *One way to interact more personally with God through Scripture is to put our name in the place of "you" or "they" in a passage. Or, if we're reading a narrative passage (a story) within the Bible, we can imagine ourselves as a participant in the scene. Encourage the group members to ask God where He would put them in what they're reading.*

5. *Answers will vary. Encourage the group to think of both grand and humble ways they might have glimpsed evidence of Him. Have them think of the natural world, the words and actions of other people, and the ways God has shaped them to be more like Himself.*

6. *Answers will vary. All too often, we base our beliefs on our present circumstances. If things are going well for us, we believe God's promise of everlasting love. If we encounter hardships, we doubt His promise. But difficult times in the life of believers are not evidence of God's detachment; rather, they are an invitation for His people to come to Him in prayer and trust Him to see them through. Difficult times compel us to rely on God. They also refine and prove one's faith. So we need the Scriptures, the community of believers, and a habit of basking in God's presence to keep us trusting in His everlasting love in hard times.*

7. *Those of us who follow Christ sometimes fear that what we've done is too much for the Lord to forgive. Or we fear that He might grudgingly forgive us, but He won't pull us close to Him in a loving embrace because we don't deserve it. However, in this passage God says that even after all the bad things His people have done, He still loves them with an everlasting love and has a plan to restore them to Himself. The sacrifice of Jesus' life is at the center of that plan.*

8. *Jesus' sacrifice on the cross is an example of His "unfailing kindness." He did it for us—even while we were still sinners (see Romans 5:8)—and did not put His own interests first. God does the same thing every day when He provides for the physical needs of His children.*

9. *Answers will vary. The more out of character it is, the more it might reflect the dramatic change that God wants to work in the lives of His followers as the depth of His love sinks into their minds and hearts. Encourage the group members to imagine being this joyful.*

10. *The image of planting vineyards and enjoying their fruit suggests purposeful labor that produces abundant results. It's an image of prosperity and good harvest, not work that is done in vain. For those of us who have trouble making ends meet, it might be like having more than enough to meet our needs. Or, if we're artists or crafters, it might be like producing exquisite work. God loves His children so much that He makes this possible.*

11. *It's important not to take worshiping God with others for granted because there are parts of the world today where Christians aren't allowed to gather for worship, and where building churches or having group worship in homes is forbidden. Also, some people's health prevents them from meeting with others for worship. Thinking about these situations should motivate us to be grateful that we do have the freedom to worship with others.*

12. *Answers will vary.*

13. *Answers will vary.*

14. *Responses will vary.*

Session 3: Abounding Love

1. *Answers will vary. Some of the group members may have recovered from an illness, received forgiveness for a fault, or even enjoyed something as simple as enough food and a safe place to sleep. There are many ways to experience God's love in tangible ways!*

2. *It can take some practice to get into the daily habit of seeing how God is demonstrating His love. If we are overly busy or stressed, we may miss all the ways that God is extending His grace and mercy to us. We can become more aware of God's goodness by slowing down, consciously looking for how He is working in our day, and then expressing thanks to Him for all He has done.*

3. *One thing that can help us choose to praise God is to reflect deeply on His boundless love. When we realize His true love for His children, whether we are in a good mood or not—or regardless of the music chosen for worship or how strong the sermon is at church—we can choose to praise the One who loves us more deeply than anyone else.*

4. *Oddly enough, choosing to worship God consistently helps us feel what is real. Worship reminds us and reinforces in our minds what is true. Reading the Scriptures can have the same effect. We need to have the truth of God's love saturating our minds until it becomes a habit for us to think about it rather than about the things that feed our insecurity.*

5. *It's often difficult for people to leave all pretense behind and go to God because they are in the habit of putting up a public face and trying to perform for approval. So much so that they often aren't even aware of doing it! It's hard for them to trust anyone's love, including God's.*

6. *In general, it's not socially acceptable for adults to express their neediness. We're supposed to have our lives under control. Neediness is associated with childishness or being disadvantaged. But God wants us to come to Him with*

our needs—both physical and spiritual: "Ask, and it will be given to you; seek, and you will find; knock, and it will be opened to you" (Matthew 7:7).

7. This psalm lists indications of God's love for His children that include forgiveness for their sins, healing, redemption from death, satisfying their desires, renewing their youth, working justice for the oppressed, and compassion.

8. Answers will vary. The most significant for each person will probably be the one he or she feels most in need of at the moment.

9. Answers will vary. Most of the group members will likely have experienced the forgiveness of their sins, but they may be shy about discussing the specifics. That's okay. It's important to encourage them to share these stories with others so they can remember them and remember to praise God for what He has done. Remembering can reinforce faith and hope.

10. God knows how limited we are. Our lives are extremely short in His eyes—a mere blink. So He's not at all surprised that we're far less wise than He is, far less powerful than He is, and far less loving than He is. He feels compassion for our weakness. He wants to help us become more Christlike, and He knows how much grace that will take. As He trains us, He takes our weakness into account.

11. If we put our trust in Christ, we have eternal life. After our earthly bodies fall to dust, we can look forward to everlasting life with Jesus in heaven where His everlasting love is on full display. Also, even in this life we may be part of families and communities of faith that will for generations live in and benefit from the Lord's everlasting, abounding love.

12. Answers will vary.

13. Answers will vary.

14. *Responses will vary.*

Session 4: Compassionate Love

1. *Answers will vary. Hopefully, all of the group members will be able to think of a time when God or another person reached out to care for them in a time of need. If we are unaware of ever receiving compassion, it will be hard for us to treat others with compassion.*

2. *We all need compassion because we all suffer to a greater or lesser degree. And our worst affliction is sin and its habits, for which we need God's compassionate forgiveness and help to overcome. Without His compassion for us as sinners, none of us would be able to look forward to eternal life in His presence. We would all be separated from Him.*

3. *This means that the things God does for His children out of His infinite love never stop coming our way. He is constantly offering us forgiveness for our sin, companionship for our pain, and support to comfort our losses. He doesn't always cause the pain to go away easily, but He always walks through the pain with us.*

4. *Knowing that God's love for His children never fails can encourage us that none of our prayers has slipped by Him unnoticed. He keeps all His promises in His perfect way and timing. While we are waiting, He gives peace that can displace the trouble in our hearts. If we are waiting, it could be that God is preparing our hearts to receive something even greater than we imagined.*

5. *One of the meanings of "unfailing" in Isaiah 54:10 is "inexhaustible." No matter how needy we are or how many times we fail God, His supply of love for His children will never run low. Another meaning of "unfailing" is "constant." God doesn't love us more on days when we perform well, nor does He love us less when we fail badly. This might be relevant to those who are aware of their neediness or those who tend to judge themselves based on performance.*

6. *Answers will vary. For some of us, the challenge as believers is to come to God when we're acutely aware of our faults. We don't want to reveal them, even to Him—we want to hide, just like Adam and Eve in the garden. In such situations, it's invaluable to know that God has compassion for us in our faults.*

7. *The author of this passage in Lamentations states that because of the Lord's great love, "we are not consumed"—that is, all is not lost. God's compassions for His people never fail, and His faithfulness is great. No matter what we've lost, Christians still have Him. He is good to those who hope in Him. Although grief will come to us in this life, He also offers His compassion to us in full measure. He doesn't willingly bring or allow affliction on anyone.*

8. *The Bible never minimizes loss. Hope is not the denial of loss but the confidence that, for Christians, loss isn't the end of the story. When we grieve, the Bible can give us solid comfort because its writers knew what it's like to lose someone or something precious. The hope in God's compassionate love doesn't ask us to pretend that life is free of pain.*

9. *As we've seen, God's compassion doesn't mean that He will immediately restore what we've lost. It means that God is with His children in their losses and is providing enough of what they need for them to continue on with a meaningful life. The poet has lost a lot, but he hasn't lost everything because he's still alive to do meaningful things. In the same way, if we are followers of Christ, we can have courage and hope no matter what happens, because we have an intimate relationship with a compassionate and unfailing God.*

10. *To say, "The Lord is my portion," is to say that as long as we have the Lord, we haven't lost everything that matters. He alone is enough to make life worth living. Waiting for God means waiting with hope and trust in Him. This type of waiting isn't demanding, but it also isn't passive or helpless. With this kind of waiting, we go about life not paralyzed, not in despair, but with a quiet expectation that God will bring something good out of the disaster.*

11. *Nothing happens in this world that God doesn't allow—and nothing catches Him by surprise. However, at the same time, we need to know that He grieves when we grieve. This will help us move toward Him when we suffer rather than moving away from Him in anger and bitterness. Remembering that He is compassionate will allow us to more fully benefit from His compassion.*

12. *Answers will vary.*

13. *Answers will vary.*

14. *Responses will vary.*

Session 5: Healing Love

1. *Answers will vary. The goal here is to get the group's longings for healing out in the open, and also to better get to know one another. Some people might want to share personal information, so be prepared to make your group a safe place to hear these things. As the leader, you can help in this process if you go first. Think of something for which you would personally like healing. If you share about a healing request for someone else, nobody may take the risk of sharing something about themselves.*

2. *Answers will vary. Again, the point here is for the group members to get to know one another and get comfortable opening up to one another. Encourage them not to tell long stories.*

3. *By this point in the study, hopefully group members know each other well enough to open up a bit about the things they don't take to God in prayer. The reading gives several possible reasons—being embarrassed about these things, being so used to them that they don't think of them, and so on. See if you can help people identify what they're not praying about.*

4. *Answers will vary, but the process requires going to Jesus in prayer day* *after day and asking Him to touch us in the area of our shame, our loneliness, or our physical ailment. Praying in a group is also helpful, because Scripture says that God moves in the faith of the gathered community. We shouldn't expect to pray about something once as followers of Christ and then assume it will all be better right away—one and done (see Luke 19:1–9). Most things take time in His presence.*

5. *Answers will vary, but one practice that can certainly help us lean on Jesus is to schedule time each day to be alone in His presence. We put aside the things we're anxious about and take them to God in prayer. This can be difficult to do at first, but over time we will find that this daily "appointment" with God is one that we look forward to keeping.*

6. *As we read in John 1:4–5, "In him was life, and that life was the light of all mankind. The light shines in the darkness, and the darkness has not overcome it." Light suggests power, warmth, and clarity of vision. God's presence brings all of these traits into His followers' lives.*

7. *The most obvious answer is that Jesus showed His love for the leper and the bleeding woman by caring enough to heal them. But beyond that, He was moved with pity—compassion—and fearlessly touched these individuals. Lepers could have disfigured faces and a stench about them, but Jesus didn't recoil from any of that. As for the woman, Jesus paused in His busy day to have a face-to-face encounter with her. He called her "daughter" and praised her faith. He wasn't put off by her malady or the fact that she was a woman.*

8. *Both the leper and the bleeding woman had good reasons to fear rejection. They were both considered unclean and outcasts in their society. They weren't supposed to make requests of someone important like a religious teacher. Also, they could well have doubted Jesus' power to heal them with a touch since even physicians couldn't help them. But both of them chose to have faith in His power and His love for those who were at the bottom of the social ladder.*

9. *No one is wholly and permanently healed in this life. We will all die of something—even Christians—unless Jesus comes back first. Even so, we would prefer a partial healing now instead of a shortened life or one marred by a major illness. But God doesn't give even that partial healing to everyone—and He doesn't always tell us the reasons why. His healings are demonstrations of His power so that we can have faith, but He wants those who aren't healed to also display His power in the midst of suffering. He wants each of us to grow strong in faith and have our faith in the spotlight because we trust Him even when we don't get what we want.*

10. *For Jesus, healing was a person-to-person, relational thing, not a work of magic. He is not a genie that we can use or call on—He is a person who wants to be known and loved. Love is relational, never merely functional. Jesus loves us and wants relationship with us.*

11. *Answers will vary. Offer confidentiality to your group to make it a safe place for people to be honest. Some members will have vivid memories of prayers that were not answered in the way they desired. It's important for them to recognize that Jesus is good even when we don't understand everything He does, and that He cares very personally and deeply for each of us.*

12. *Answers will vary.*

13. *Answers will vary.*

14. *Responses will vary.*

Session 6: Rooted in Love

1. *Answers will vary. God can revolutionize a life when we are teens or adults, but it's a lot easier to connect with God's love if we had a healthy, loving environment growing up.*

2. *For most of us, our childhood experience of our parents' love has a big effect—for good or for bad—on how we view the love of our heavenly Father. But the wonder of God's grace is that He can even overcome childhood deprivation and teach us to root ourselves in Him and His love.*

3. *Close friends and family may disappoint us at times by not keeping their word or commitments toward us. The first part of the solution in overcoming these disappointments is to immerse ourselves in the biblical truth that God and His Word can always be trusted. Unlike in our human relationships, God never breaks His promises. It is impossible for Him. Additionally, we need to ask God's Holy Spirit to empower us to know this love that surpasses knowledge.*

4. *Answers will vary. The danger in viewing ourselves differently from the way God sees us is that it can lead to us potentially believing a lie—especially if we see ourselves as worthless or hopeless. Believers in Christ can change this false perception by soaking in God's presence and learning the truth of what He says about us in His Word. For example, as we read in 1 Peter 2:9, "You are a chosen generation, a royal priesthood, a holy nation, His own special people, that you may proclaim the praises of Him who called you out of darkness into His marvelous light" (NKJV).*

5. *Knowing about God is knowing the information the Bible provides about Him. We know that He is everywhere, all-powerful, all-loving, all-wise . . . and so on. This is important information to have, but actually knowing Him as our Lord and Savior goes further. It is a personal connection. A Father-son or Father-daughter relationship. We experience His love personally instead of just reading and hearing about it. This moves the truth of His love from our head to our heart.*

6. *Answers will vary. The goal here is to give the group members a chance to share their successes and difficulties in making time for God each day. This will give them opportunity to receive help from each other and gain motivation to make time for Him.*

7. Being "rooted" in God's love means to be so confident and aware of His love for us that we aren't thrown into doubt by negative circumstances that come our way. It means to find our soul's nourishment from His love rather than from earthly substitutes.

8. One of the main evidences that a believer is rooted in God's love is that he or she treats others with this same kind of self-sacrificial, generous love. Another evidence would be that he or she doesn't panic when bad things happen.

9. Many believers today are unaware of the activity of God's Spirit in their lives. If we lack that sense of rootedness in God's love, maybe the strengthening of the Spirit is something we need to pray for persistently. This strengthening from the Spirit is available to all who come to Christ and accept Him as their Lord and Savior.

10. As human beings, we will never fully understand the vastness of God's love; but if we are believers in Christ, we can grow in our understanding as we open ourselves to help from Him. This is something else the Holy Spirit will do for us if we ask Him. We can ask the Holy Spirit to help us know and experience God's love more widely, more deeply.

11. Paul says that God's power is able to do far more for His children than they could possibly ask or imagine. As believers, we may think we're a long way from being rooted in God's love, but His power can shorten the distance if we trust Him.

12. Answers will vary.

13. Answers will vary.

14. Responses will vary.

Session 7: Fearless Love

1. *Answers will vary, but it's important to acknowledge that fearlessness comes more easily to some people than to others. In naturally more risk-averse people, fearless love is more obviously the work of God.*

2. *Answers will vary. Note that there's nothing inherently more godly in being a risk taker. Some people take foolish risks or selfish risks. What we're working toward is a fearlessness about love because we don't fear mistakes and God's disapproval.*

3. *God revealed His love for us by noticing everything about us from before we were born, as Jeremiah 1:5 says. He orchestrated circumstances to help us see our need of Him, provided people in our lives who told us about Him, and His Spirit continually compels those of us who are His followers to serve and obey the course He has set for our lives. The fact that we are participating in this Bible study is the result of years of God lavishing His love on us.*

4. *It is important to contemplate the many ways God has shown His love for us because it motivates us to love Him and love others. It keeps us from walking through life feeling discontented because people don't treat us the way we want to be treated. Instead of being resentful or disappointed, we live in gratitude, and that helps us be more loving. Also, when we're secure in God's love, we're freer to focus on loving others fearlessly.*

5. *Embracing Jesus' love can help us see that we don't have to perform well for God to keep loving us. And His love is the most important nourishment that our souls need. So, while there may be unpleasantness if we make a mistake, we are secure in having what we most need.*

6. *If we're hard on ourselves when we make a mistake, it means we've internalized a critical voice somewhere along the way, perhaps made up of all the critical voices we have heard since childhood. We may even think that* voice is the voice of God—but it isn't. God invites us to know we are loved even though we're flawed. He invites us to let the mistake go, try to fix it if possible, and then move on to the next decision or action we need to take.

7. Love is the essence of who God is—not romantic love, but self-sacrificing and self-giving love. God naturally overflows with this kind of love because it is a core aspect of His character—He is someone who loves, and everything He does is loving, just as everything He does is holy and right and good. The greatest expression of this type of love is found in John 3:16: "For God so loved the world that He gave His only begotten Son, that whoever believes in Him should not perish but have everlasting life" (NKJV).

8. God showed His love for us by sending His beloved Son to die on our behalf, in penalty for our sins, so that we could avoid an eternal death sentence for our sins. This is different from the intense romantic emotions two people sometimes feel for each other. God didn't simply have an intense feeling and desire for us—He was willing to give up the life of His only Son to restore the relationship with us that had been broken through sin. He calls us to accept that sacrifice and follow Him with our lives.

9. Love comes from God and should naturally flow from Him to others through His followers. For the believer in Christ, loving others is a sign of knowing God and being born of God. If we love one another as He instructs, God "completes" His love in us. In other words, experiencing love from God bears fruit, producing love for others and practical opportunities of expressing it. If that doesn't happen, something is amiss.

10. We shouldn't chase the "feeling" of being loved by God, because feelings come and go. Instead, we have to be intentional in our efforts to love others— even the difficult people in our lives to whom we don't necessarily want to show love. The focus needs to be on actively offering to others the love that God gave us, not necessarily on feeling loved.

11. *Answers will vary. As the group leader, you might want to lead off the discussion by talking about how giving of yourself to others actually draws you closer to God and alleviates fear of Him. Try to give concrete examples from your own experience.*

12. *Answers will vary.*

13. *Answers will vary.*

14. *Responses will vary.*

Session 8: Persevering Love

1. *Answers will vary. The goal of this question is to help group members further deepen their connection with each other while giving them a chance to reflect on their early days. Many of us, as we look back on our younger years, may believe that our actions at the time made us difficult for other people to love. Whether or not this is true, we can always know that God loves us—even at our very worst (see Romans 5:8).*

2. *We all get impatient at times. Driving, in particular, often brings out the impatience even in people who are otherwise naturally easygoing and calm, though there are certainly other "patience-challenging" situations as well. Urge the group to think of other instances.*

3. *Answers will vary, but being open to God involves carving out the time to be with Him so a relationship of trust can develop. A good Scripture to pray to open ourselves fully to Him is the one found in the reading—"Search me, God, and know my heart; test me and know my anxious thoughts. See if there is any offensive way in me, and lead me in the way everlasting" (Psalm 139:23–24). We can then tell Him whatever is on our minds and listen to His response to us through the Scriptures. It's also important for us to try to become aware of the pretenses we wear with other people so we can lay them aside when we're with God.*

4. *God sees us as we are now—and still loves us. Yet He also knows who we were fully meant to be—and He wants that person to fully come forth. He isn't angry at us for not yet being that way, and He can never love us more than He loves us now. However, it is precisely because He loves us that He longs to see us become whole and fully able to love Him and others.*

5. *Answers will vary. When we feel impatient toward someone, it's helpful to ask God to enable us to see that person the way He does. Something that gets in the way of our patience with people is an excessive focus on our own productivity. Task orientation makes us continually in a hurry to get things done—and more prone to be brusque with others. Real love can't be rushed.*

6. *Trials don't automatically help us grow in patience—we each determine whether we grow more like Jesus or push ourselves away from Him in anger and bitterness. If we move toward Him, casting our grief and fear at His feet, our patience will grow. This will have other benefits, such as the ability to empathize with others in the midst of their sufferings.*

7. *God knows our strengths and our limitations. He knows how far we have to go before we will measure up to the standard of love He has set for us. And He doesn't reject His children when we fail. Knowing this frees us to try to love as we should with His Spirit's help, even if we fall short again and have to keep on trying.*

8. *Jesus shows the kind of love Paul describes in 1 Corinthians 13:4–8 by treating us with patience, waiting as long as it takes for us to grow into the loving habits He intends for us. He doesn't lash out in anger when we take a long time to "get it" or fall short and grieve Him. He is kind, lavishing us with food, shelter, and the other things we need. Of course, His ultimate act of loving kindness toward us was when He chose to die for our sins on the cross.*

9. *Romantic feelings can slip away in the face of difficulties, but real love doesn't quit when things get hard. Real love continues to seek the good of the* *other person even when the person gets sick or the money runs out. This makes real love reliable—we don't have to worry that something bad will happen and we'll be abandoned. Other people shouldn't have to worry about that from us if we truly love them with the love of God.*

10. *There are many ways to show love toward an untrustworthy person that don't involve putting ourselves in a position where others can take advantage of us. For example, maybe we have a boss who is more interested in being in control than in producing quality products or seeking what is good for employees. Love enables us to see this person honestly and treat him or her with respect while trusting God to keep us safe. We don't have to be too quick to quit the job if we sense that God wants us there for a reason or for some period of time. If God wants us there, He will enable us to stay safe while being patient, kind, and loving toward this difficult person. Pose a few additional situations for the group to consider beyond work.*

11. *Answers will vary. Hopefully, the group members know each other well enough by now to be honest in openly discussing this question.*

12. *Answers will vary.*

13. *Answers will vary.*

14. *Responses will vary.*

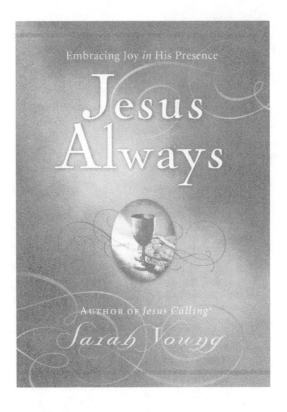

Also available in the
JESUS ALWAYS® BIBLE STUDY SERIES

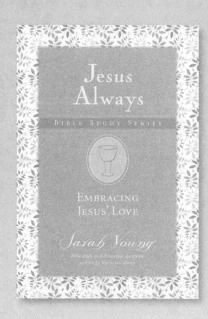

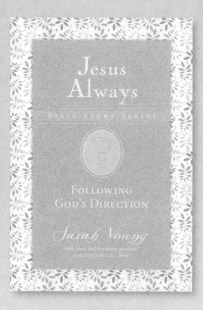

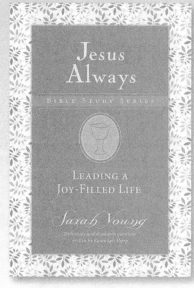

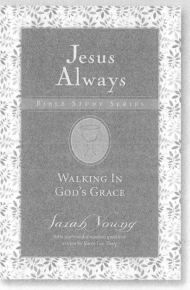

Also Available in the
Jesus Calling® Bible Study Series

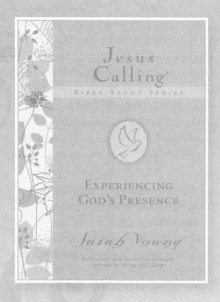

Jesus Calling®
BIBLE STUDY SERIES

EXPERIENCING
GOD'S PRESENCE

Sarah Young

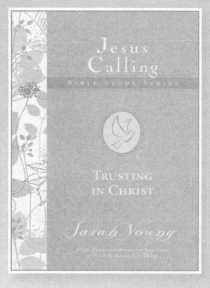

Jesus Calling
BIBLE STUDY SERIES

TRUSTING
IN CHRIST

Sarah Young

Jesus Calling®
BIBLE STUDY SERIES

RECEIVING
CHRIST'S HOPE

Sarah Young

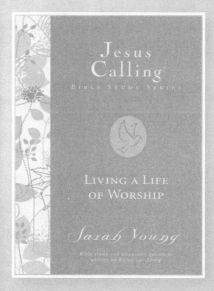

Jesus Calling®
BIBLE STUDY SERIES

LIVING A LIFE
OF WORSHIP

Sarah Young

Also Available in the
Jesus Calling® Bible Study Series

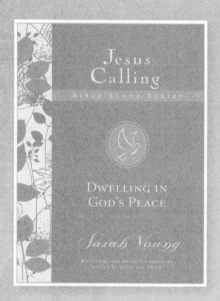

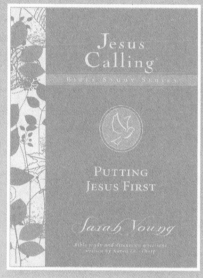

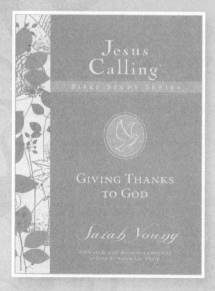

If you liked reading this book, you may enjoy
these other titles by *Sarah Young*

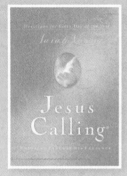

Jesus Calling®
Hardcover

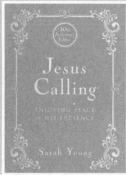

**Jesus Calling® 10th
Anniversary Edition**
Bonded Leather

Peace in His Presence:
Favorite Quotations from Jesus Calling®
Padded Hardcover

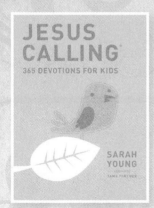

Jesus Calling® for Kids
Hardcover

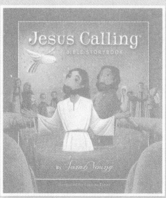

Jesus Calling® Bible Storybook
Hardcover

Jesus Calling® for Little Ones
Board Book